D1493371

Creating Pictures with Calligraphy

xb
Christe benedic ~ a mediaeval scribe's symbol for deliverance from error ~

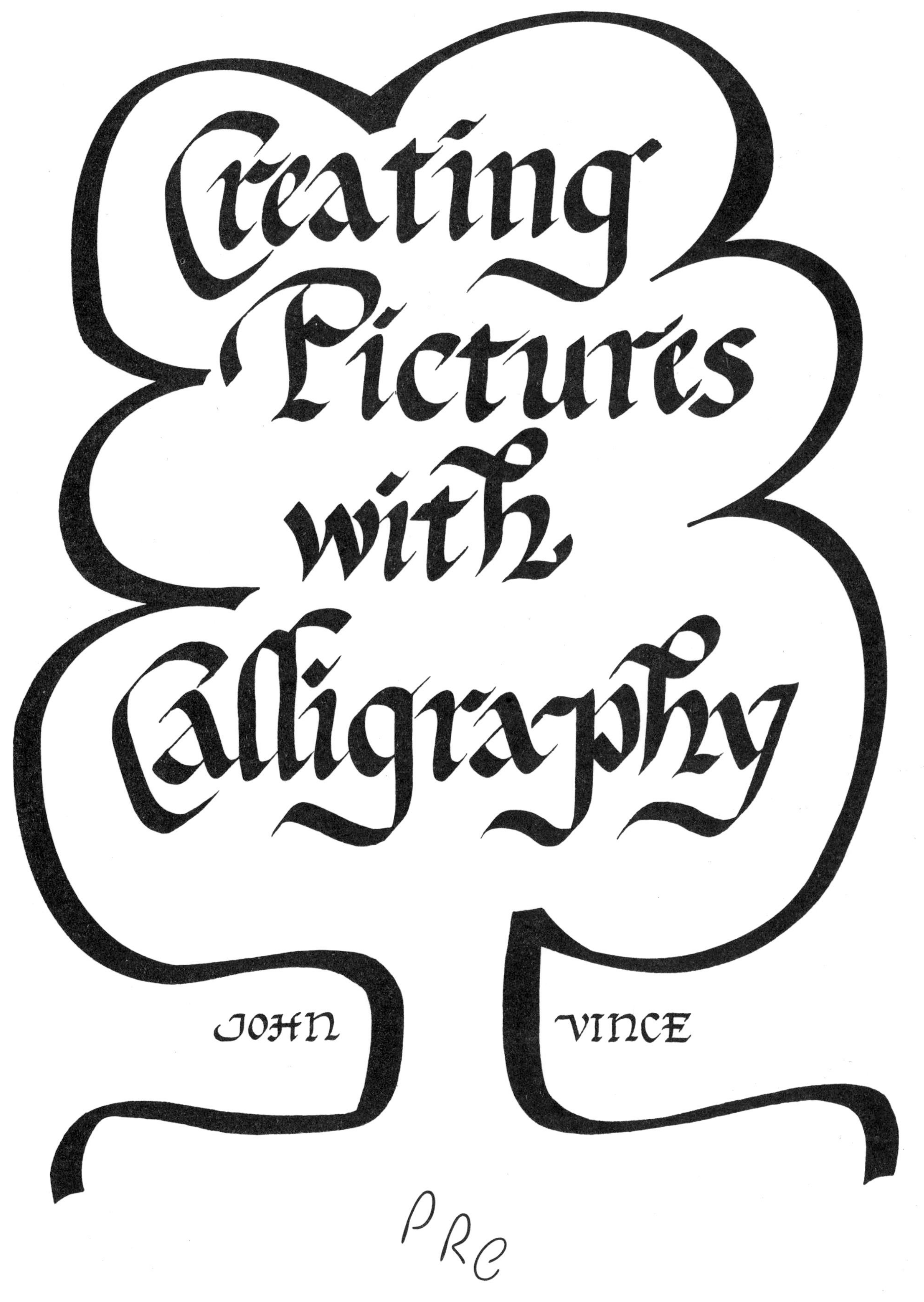
Creating
Pictures
with
Calligraphy
JOHN VINCE
PRC

First published in Great Britain
1987

This edition published 1992 by
The Promotional Reprint Company Limited,
exclusively for Bookmart Limited, Desford
Road, Enderby, Leicester, UK and
Angus & Robertson Bookshops in Australia.

ISBN 1 85648 046 1

Printed in Czechoslovakia
50921

~CONTENTS~

Introduction	7
Writing Tools	9
Posture	10
The Writing Surface	12
Alphabets	14
Capitals	18
Numerals	20
Notes on the Exercises	21
Abbreviations	21
Getting Started	24
Picture Ideas	32
Applications	130
Borders	148
Tailpiece	153
Notes on Useful Pens	154
Bibliography	156
Index	158

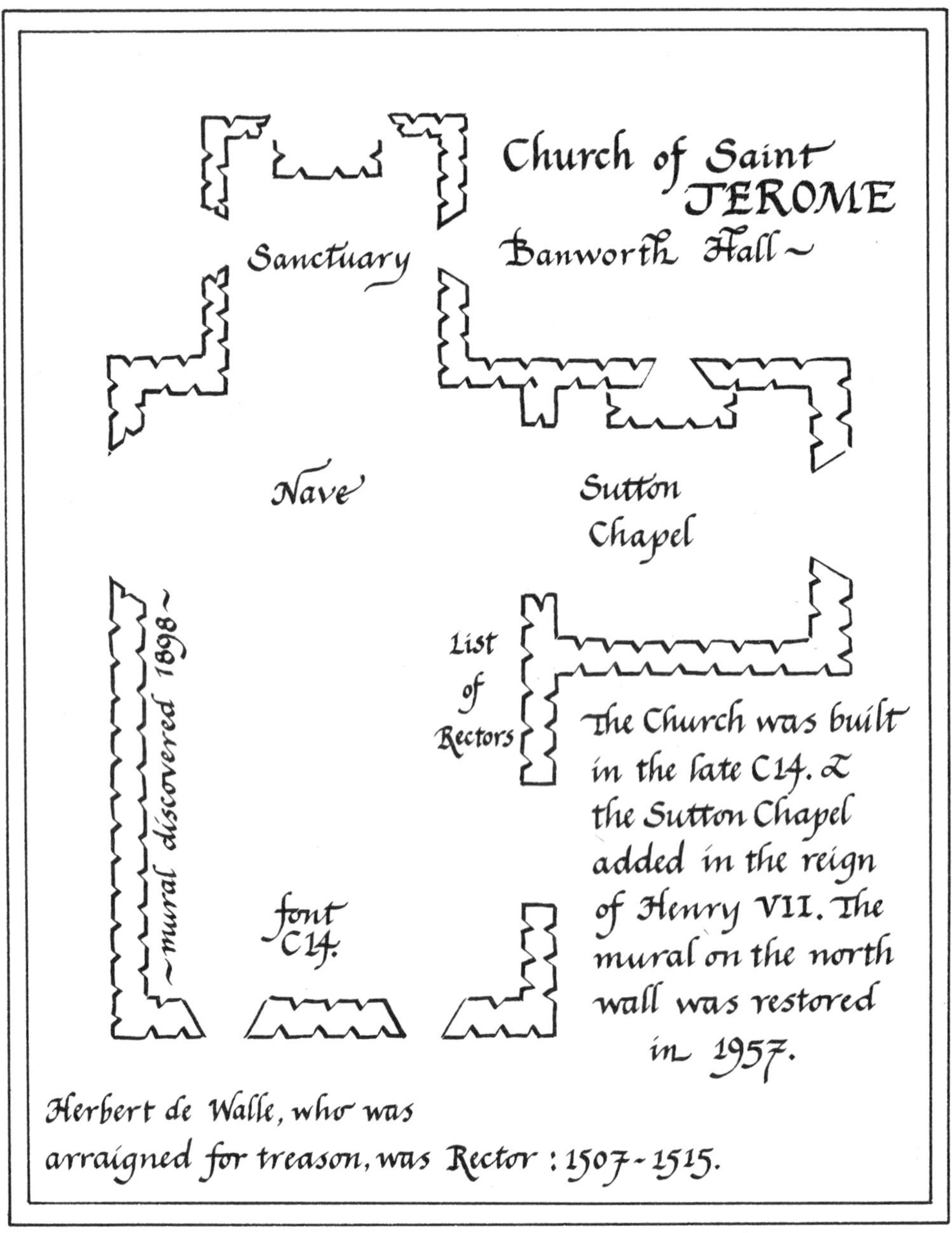

Church of Saint
JEROME
Banworth Hall ~
Sanctuary
Nave
Sutton
Chapel
~mural discovered 1898~
List
of
Rectors
font
C14.
The Church was built
in the late C14. &
the Sutton Chapel
added in the reign
of Henry VII. The
mural on the north
wall was restored
in 1957.
Herbert de Walle, who was
arraigned for treason, was Rector : 1507 - 1515.

See MAPS ~
page 142

INTRODUCTION

For some five thousand years mankind has been making use of symbols to express ideas & convey information. We owe a great debt to the ancient Egyptians who through their secret writings provided a starting-point for our modern alphabets. The first writing was in the form of pictures. The Egyptian hieroglyphs, in time, became the hieratic script which was recorded on fragile papyrus. From these sacred forms the demotic script was derived & the mystery of writing became secular property.

This book borrows from the ancient idea of pictorial forms. The symbols we now use, & call letters, have to be arranged into words, & these words have to be set in a sequence to make sense in a sentence. Experts in the teaching of reading tell us that the SHAPE of a word enables a reader to identify its sound & meaning. MEANING was conveyed by the writers of hieroglyphics, & in the pictorial texts of the American Indians, by shape alone. A definable shape is still a powerful element in our lives & it can convey a significant idea like

SOLIDARNOŚĆ

At first sight some of the designs here may look complex. However, they are all composed of simple elements. They are well within the capacity of anyone who has worked through the earlier exercises, but they will demand more time & concentration. The best progress in calligraphy is slow progress, so do not hurry.

The illustrations of most of the designs – on odd-numbered pages – are reproduced exactly the same size as the originals. Each page of instruction & commentary has been reduced to 90% of its original size. This has the effect of making a sharper image on the page. An example of reduction is shown on page 144.

The shapes in this book are made with a chisel-edged pen. The form & words used as its components help to contribute to the idea or statement a particular shape can make. The examples shown are not specifically ends in themselves, although they could be so. They are presented as starting-points for your own excursions into a field of calligraphy that is not the secret preserve of expert craftsmen. Writing should be a pleasure & there is no reason why a note for the milkman should not be given an elegant form in its own right. In an age when so much written material is mechanically produced in the sterile layouts derived from a 'printout', individuality has almost been lost. The personal touch, however, is perhaps now more than ever appreciated in the face of arid technology. People are more important than processors & people alone can make meaningful marks upon life's page.

Those who choose to follow up some of the ideas suggested here in their own way will need to search out other books & explore their surroundings for shapes that can be translated into a written form. Architecture & landscape can generate many useful ideas once you acquire a habit of looking.

There are no absolutely right or wrong answers in calligraphy. The result is what you wish to be. This is not to say that we should not try to improve our fluency or technique, but we decide on our own aims & progress.

Apart from personal satisfaction, those who engage in calligraphy will need to become lost in their own concentration for you cannot write well if you or your hand are tense. Calligraphy then, as some people have discovered, has a great potential as a therapeutic device in a world crowded with other tensions. Writing, & that metaphysical contact between the mind, pen & paper, should, above all, be a matter of pleasure & serenity.

May you have a good journey & in discovering an almost lost art discover other things as well.

WRITING TOOLS

The writer's most important tool is the pen. A beginner should start with one pen & a broad nib. An edged pen can make a thick & thin stroke. These are formed by the way in which the pen is held. As you write, the pen angle should remain constant.

45°

THE PEN GRIP VIEWED FROM ABOVE

The pen grip is important. Hold the pen between thumb & forefinger, & rest the lower part of the pen on the middle finger. In its turn the middle is supported by the two other fingers.

Hold the pen gently. A tight grip will tire the hand & diminish fluency.

Viewed from the side the pen should be held at about 45° to the writing surface.

THICK

THIN

A

B

45°

HORIZONTAL

The edge of the pen nib should be held at an angle of 45° to the horizontal line. When the pen moves in direction of → A it makes a THICK stroke. When the pen moves in the direction of → B it will make a THIN stroke.

POSTURE

Once you have mastered the pen grip pay attention to your sitting posture. This, like your pen grip, should be relaxed & comfortable. Some people prefer to write on a flat desk, but others like a sloping surface. The diagram shows a suitable posture. Some writers are tempted to bend reverentially over their work. A straight back is, however, the best working stance.

The degree of slope is a matter of personal choice. Try a board, supported by books, as a writing surface. When the most suitable slope has been decided wooden blocks may be fixed to the underside of the board so that its slope is always constant. Remember to place your writing sheet on an underlay – see p. 12.

• SIDE VIEW OF WRITING POSTURE •

Get used to a comfortable posture & the sloping surface. It is important to have good illumination. Light from in front or from the left hand side, for the right-handed, is best. The use of an adjustable is helpful.

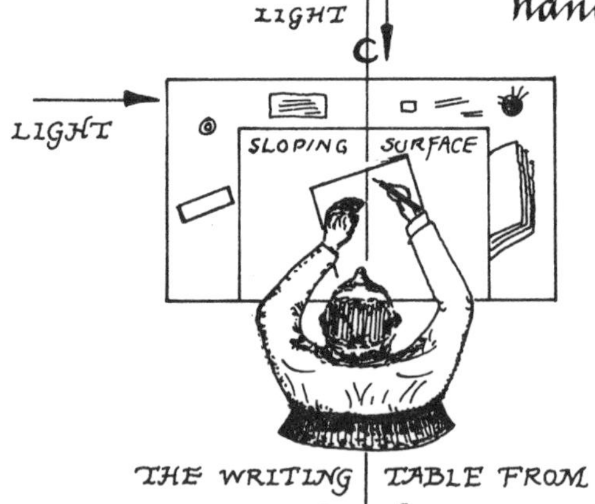

THE WRITING TABLE FROM ABOVE

The sloping surface should be large enough to give support for your forearm.

For fluent work a relaxed pen grip & a relaxed posture is very important. Do not try to rush your writing. Speed is not an objective.

Left-handed writers need to adopt a slightly different stance to avoid the writing hand obscuring the line of writing. A left-handed writer can acquire just as much skill as anyone.

CENTRE LINE OF BODY

30°

The key to comfort is to place the paper to the left of the body's centre line, as the diagram shows. Incline the paper at about 30° – or at an angle which is comfortable. In this position you may find it helpful to incline the head slightly to the right, but do not tense your neck muscles. Support the paper with your right hand. Some people may be more comfortable with the hand BELOW the writing hand. Decide on the position which suits you best. Always persevere!

Many novices sometimes find that the nib wants to dig into the writing surface. They check the pen grip & posture, but the problem is still present. To work effectively the nib must slide across the paper's surface. If you have trouble with a nib digging-in adjust the pen's attitude, between finger & thumb, by rotating it a few degrees.

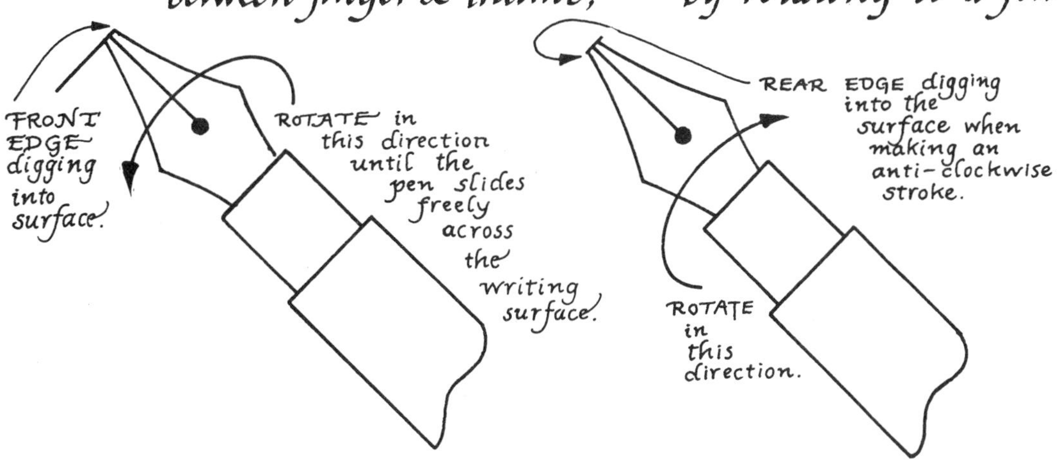
FRONT EDGE digging into surface.
ROTATE in this direction until the pen slides freely across the writing surface.
REAR EDGE digging into the surface when making an anti-clockwise stroke.
ROTATE in this direction.

THE WRITING SURFACE

When you have selected your pen you will want to get down to the business of writing. Take care to prepare a writing surface that will suit the pen you use, & the pressure you put on the paper. This should be very light. Never PRESS HARD as this will affect your fluency & tire your hand. DO NOT WRITE on a surface that is hard. The paper you write upon needs to rest on several sheets of paper. These will form a 'cushion' for the nib. This will allow the ink flow to run properly. The number of sheets you use is a matter of personal choice. Experiment with various thicknesses until you get a comfortable 'bite' from your pen.

Arrange your 'cushion' in the way shown in the diagram. Use A3 sized sheets taped to a backing card. This extra size is useful as it allows work to be rotated without falling off the backing sheets. There is also a bigger area to support the writer's hand.

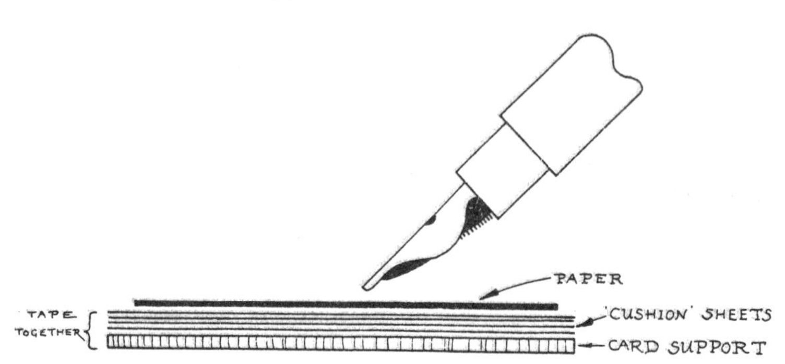

INKS ~

Different makes of pen have different ink-flow rates. Your choice of ink may also affect the ink-flow, as the thickness of inks is a variable quality. Some pens allow you to adjust the ink-flow, but most do not. Care is needed in the choice of pens and inks. If your pen delivers too much ink it will make letters which are 'heavy' in form & the thin strokes will be too wide.

An equal difficulty can arise if the pen is too dry. The quality of the letters will suffer & the nib will not flow easily across the surface of the paper. The old style inkwell or bottle can be useful for too much or too little ink. An overfull nib can be discharged by a light touch on the well; & the dry nib can be remedied by a quick dip into the ink.

After a time ink will become dry on a nib & then the flow can be restricted. Pens should be cleaned fairly often ~ notice how red ink will form crystals around a nib. Use clean cold water to clean pens. Various pen cleaners are available, but these are of most use for drawing, waterproof, inks These are not suitable for fountain pens.

Always keep your tools clean. It is a good habit to wipe nibs clean when you finish work.

PAPER ~

There are many kinds of papers available. These, like inks, vary in quality. For rough practice the thick A4 pads sold in large stationers are usually adequate, but for finished work a heavier paper is needed. Some shops sell good quality paper by weight which is made in various attractive colours. Re-cycled papers are also made in several colours and in heavy grades.

Layout paper is a very useful addition to the worktable. It is thin enough for you to use it to trace rough designs. Layout paper is often absorbent & rough ideas could be worked out with an edged carpenter's pencil or a felt pen.

ALPHABETS

abcdefghijklmnopqrstuvwxyz

The alphabet which works harder than any other is the one shown above. We call this alphabet the minuscule or lower case alphabet (the latter is a printer's term). Minuscules – Latin: minuscula = rather less – are obviously more numerous than capitals, the majuscules, as a glance at these pages will show. It is of some importance to master the minuscules, & in this chapter we will look at the way in which the letters are formed. There are three kinds of minuscule: those which are one letter high – the 'a' size –; those which ASCEND – the 'b' size –; & those which DESCEND – the 'g' size. Each of these groups have sub-divisions as shown.

First of all remember the correct pen grip & posture. When held correctly the pen will make this pattern VVVV.

These letters are made with anticlockwise strokes.

a c e o

Five pen widths tall.

These letters are made with vertical strokes & arches.

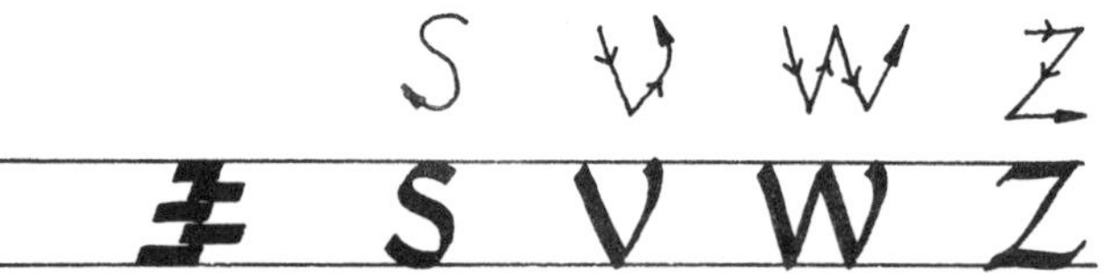

These letters are made with a continuous stroke.

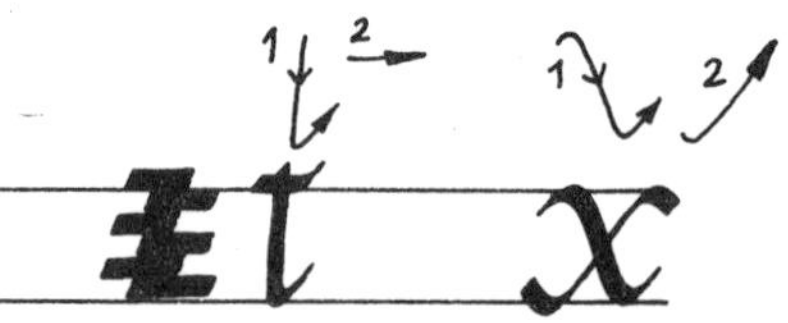

Two stroke letters.

't' is SIX PENWIDTHS TALL

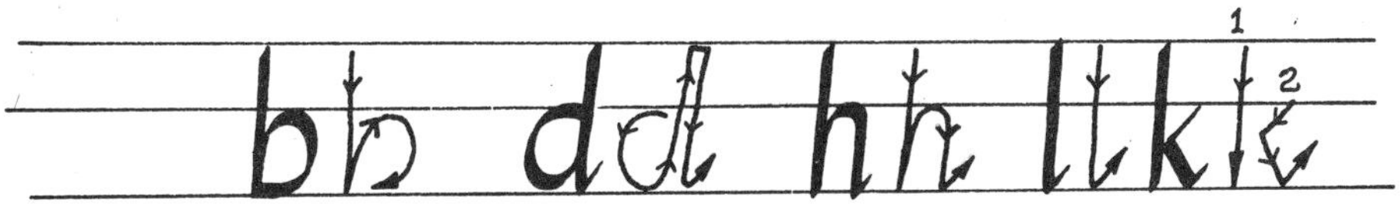

b b d d h h l l k k

Ascending letters are usually nine pen widths tall.
Descending letters are the same size.

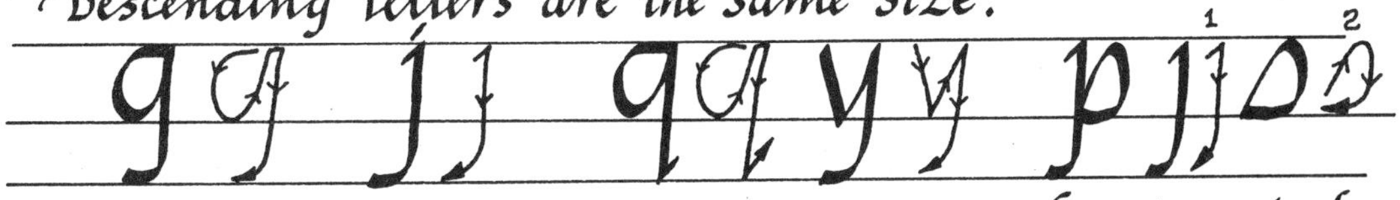

g g j j q q y y p p p p

~has two strokes~

This letter is an ascender & a descender — f — The second stroke is at 'a' height.

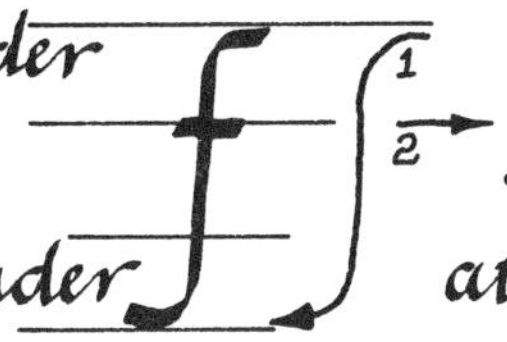

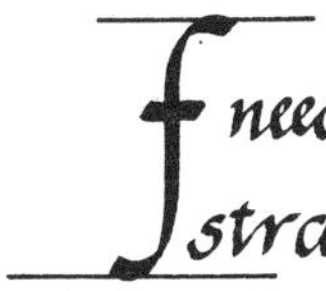

f needs a straight back.

The tailstroke of 'f' is sometimes made longer than g j q y ~

~ JOINS ~

The ITALIC style does not require ALL letters to be joined. It is important to distinguish between letters which can be joined & those which should not.

These letters ARE NOT joined to letters which FOLLOW THEM.

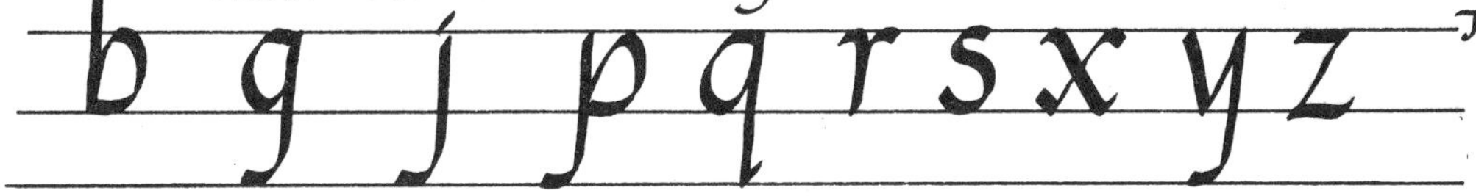

b g j p q r s x y z

These letters should not be joined to any letter which precedes them.

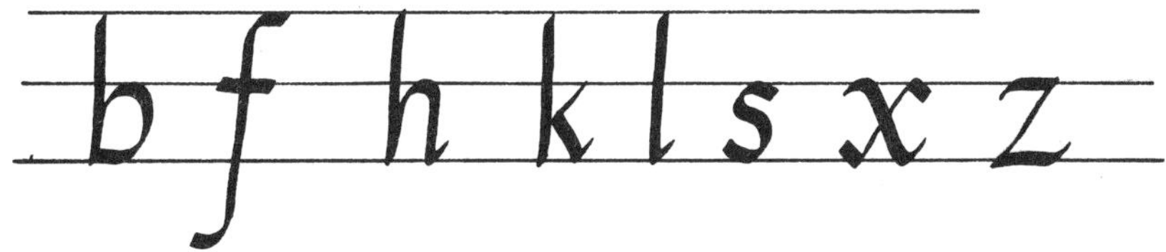

There are some words which appear to have joined letters which break these rules. These are FALSE JOINS ~ they are made by adding a final flick stroke to an 'unjoined' letter.

Thus unjoined letters can make certain words look like this.

sha shall minuscules

The flick stroke on the 'a' overlaps the space to be occupied by the 'l'

overlapping strokes make a false join

no join from the 's'

flick stroke which links 'a' to 'l'

blacksmith yellow helix

false join

false join

false joins

false join

extended stroke to form half of 'x'

~ DOTS ~ COMMAS ~ STOPS ~

One of the refinements the writer must develop can make a difference to the appearance of a piece of writing. A dot can be made in two ways. You can use a square stop ♦ which is made with a part of the broad downstroke thus \ ⁝ stop ....

The alternative stop is a flick stroke made from part of a thin upstroke. You must make a personal choice about the dots you decide to use. Some writers use an upward flick to dot an 'i' & a square dot for a full stop.

ironing is a special item with

ironing is a special item with

For those who use the Italic hand for their everyday writing the flick stroke is probably a fraction quicker. It is a matter of personal taste. Practise this basic alphabet using a broad nib. Add variety to your trial letters by using contrasting coloured felt pens ~ see page 154.

When you have mastered the letters of this basic alphabet you will be ready to develop a few embellishments to add a touch of fluency to your work.

This basic alphabet

abcdefghijklmnopqrstuvwxyz.

can become

abcd∂efghijklmnopqqrrstuvwxyz.

The differences between these alphabets is slight but the second has a distinct visual impact. These variations mostly concern the ascenders. They can have alternative renderings as these examples show.

b c+l=d h l+<=k

another d from two strokes c + l = d

a fast letter made with a backward movement

made with a continuous stroke

an embellishment with several uses

h k e ee no pen lift d no pen lift

An exaggerated stroke which can "fill-up" a line.

1 2

two versions of q

CAPITALS

The use of the capital letter predates the minuscule and it can take many forms. This alphabet is a simple one based upon the time-honoured ROMAN exemplars. Most people expect capitals to be much larger than minuscules but in a handwritten form this was not always so. In his classic book 'LA OPERINA' the master (Ludovico Vicentino - Arrighi) does not always make his capitals dominate the minuscules. The shape of these majuscules distinguishes them from the other letters, & there are good reasons for making them about six penwidths tall. This will give them a condensed appearance. Most capitals will look satisfactory if they are slightly smaller than the ascenders.

ABCDEFGHIJKL

CAPITALS SHOULD BE UPRIGHT

MNOPQRSTUVWXYZ

This basic alphabet is constructed in the following manner.

A B C D E F G H

I J K L M N O P Q R

S T U V W X Y Z

Practise this alphabet with your broad pen and with some felt pens of different widths or colours.

This alphabet is not confined to the fixed height of the basic capitals on the previous page. These letters are best made with quickly executed strokes and a degree of feeling.

A A B B C C D D

D D E E F F G G H H

H H I I J J K K K

L L L L M M M M

N N N N O O P P

P P Q Q R R R R

S S T T T T T U U

V V V W X X X Y Y Z Z

NUMERALS

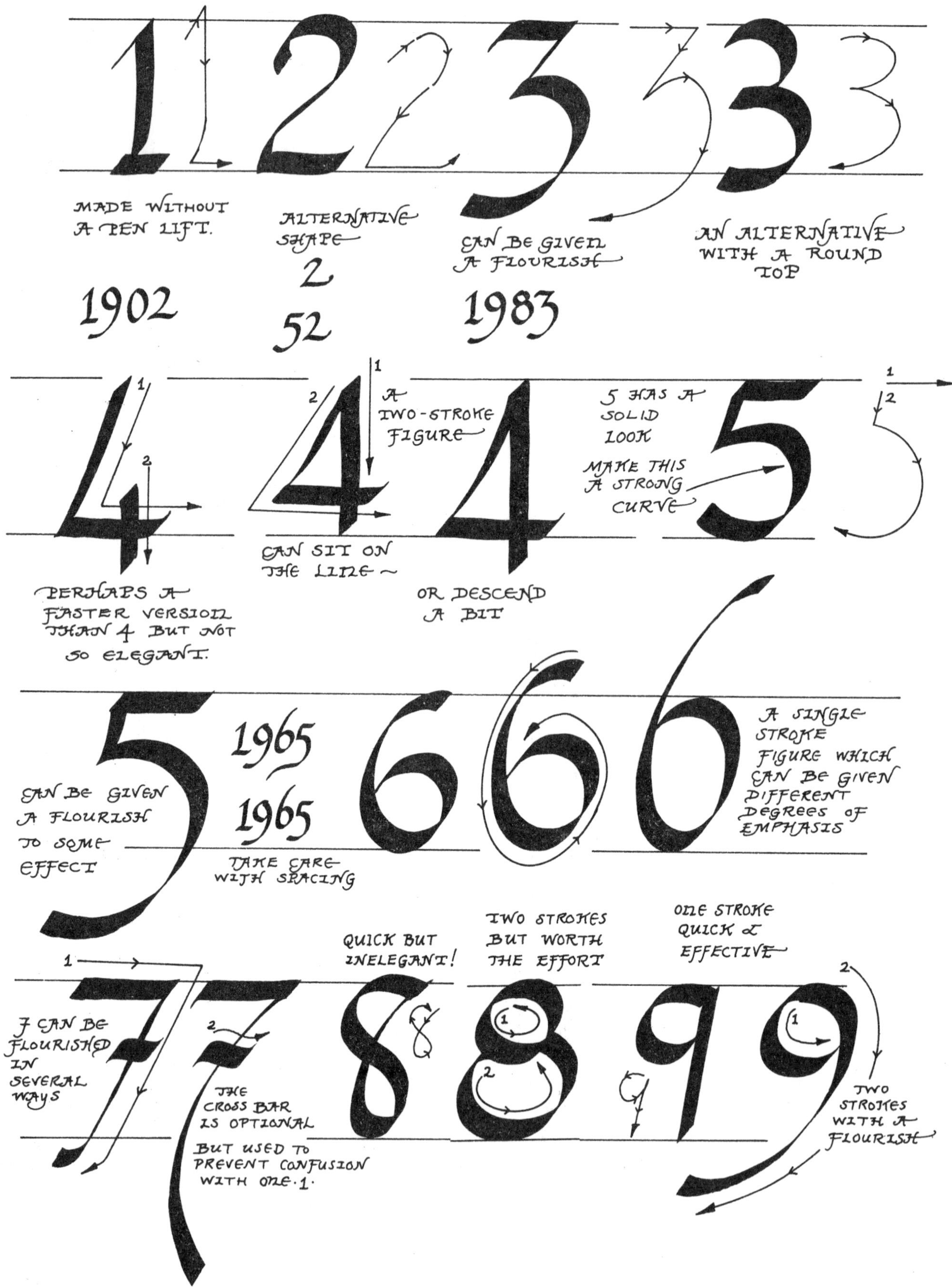
MADE WITHOUT A PEN LIFT.
ALTERNATIVE SHAPE
2
52
1902
CAN BE GIVEN A FLOURISH
1983
AN ALTERNATIVE WITH A ROUND TOP
A TWO-STROKE FIGURE
5 HAS A SOLID LOOK
MAKE THIS A STRONG CURVE
CAN SIT ON THE LINE ~
OR DESCEND A BIT
PERHAPS A FASTER VERSION THAN 4 BUT NOT SO ELEGANT.
1965
1965
CAN BE GIVEN A FLOURISH TO SOME EFFECT
TAKE CARE WITH SPACING
A SINGLE STROKE FIGURE WHICH CAN BE GIVEN DIFFERENT DEGREES OF EMPHASIS
QUICK BUT INELEGANT!
TWO STROKES BUT WORTH THE EFFORT
ONE STROKE QUICK & EFFECTIVE
7 CAN BE FLOURISHED IN SEVERAL WAYS
THE CROSS BAR IS OPTIONAL
BUT USED TO PREVENT CONFUSION WITH ONE · 1 ·
TWO STROKES WITH A FLOURISH

~ NOTES ON THE EXERCISES ~

The next ten pages ~ up to 31 ~ contain simple designs which should be worked through first. Each of the exercises has a patterned outline. This shape should be sketched lightly in pencil first ~ a pale blue one would be best. Then make the outline pattern. Work clockwise around the outline. When this has been completed the next task is to 'fit' the words inside the shape. Concentrate upon the letter shapes & the joins shown. Try to avoid clashing ascending or descending strokes together. It is worthwhile to make a second version of each exercise by introducing colour.

From p.32 onwards more detailed instructions are given for each exercise. The earlier examples are made with a single pen. Gradually two or more pens are employed as more elements are added to the designs.

ABBREVIATIONS · The pen/s used for a given design are shown. Relative sizes of letters are described in pen widths. Thus ~ 'a' = three p.w.h. indicates a minuscule 'a' three pen widths high. 'A' = five p.w.h. defines a capital five pen widths tall.

Remember to work slowly at the speed which suits you.

KEEPING STRAIGHT: It is very easy for a line of writing to go uphill or downhill. Some people find that a ruled sheet placed underneath the paper is sufficient to provide a guide. You should prepare several sheets to suit different pen widths. These guidelines are best made with a technical pen which makes a line of equal width. The distance between the writing lines can be varied for different effects.

USING A GRID: Many of the designs which follow can be written within a grid which provides straight lines in two directions. You may find it easier to use squared paper to begin with as this can be a help to accuracy. The most useful squares are 5mm. in size. These can be obtained in A4 pads from most stationers. The grid is very useful for laying out a border.

TURNING THE PAPER: In making many of the designs, you will have to rotate the paper. When writing around a curved line keep your hand on the inside of the curve. It is much more difficult to write around the outside of a curve, although this can be achieved. As you write around a curve turn the paper quite frequently. Avoid contorting the hand to keep to a curve's profile.

SMUDGES: It is always irritating when a piece of work becomes smudged. Try to avoid the use of blotting-paper as this often makes the area of damage greater. Liquid paper can cover a multitude of sins, but do allow the ink to dry before you apply it. The offending word or letter can then be corrected.

REPAIRS: Some smudges are too big to correct with liquid paper. If a disaster occurs you need not rewrite the whole piece. Make a patch instead. Place a piece of new paper over the damaged word. Write out the word again, & allow it to dry. Then cut out the word so that it will 'fit' into the surrounding text as the diagram shows.

frequent

COPY OUT THE WORD.

frequent

TRIM TO 'FIT' SURROUNDING TEXT.

You will find it easier to place a patch in position with a pair of tweezers. When you have prepared the repair, test its position within the text & then paste its reverse side before fitting it into the damaged area.

BLUE PENCILS: At several places in the text a reference is made to the use of a blue pencil. There is a practical reason for this. If you use a design for reproduction, by a printer or by making a photocopy, any blue construction lines will not register. Always use a very pale blue, not a dark blue pencil.

DIP PENS: Although fountain pens were used for almost all the designs in this book, dip pens are still very useful tools. Designs, like the landscapes on page 140, can be enhanced by using a dip pen. The broad nibs with reservoirs can make strong lines, but you need to take care not to over-fill the pen. Dip pens & reservoirs should be cleaned after use, & not left to accumulate a deposit of dry ink. There are some very good inks available in the Osmiroid & Rotring ranges. Inks can be diluted with distilled water & many different colours obtained by mixing inks together.

WELSH WORDS make frequent appearances in the text. They contain unusual combinations of letters & therefore demand extra concentration, & a slower rate of working. The same consideration would apply to any other language ~ e.g. Latin. To assist the rhythm of writing other letter combinations are used ~ e.g. eaea ... ememem ... etc.

N.B. ~ An OSMIROID BROAD PEN was used for all the exercises up to page 65. ~

KEYHOLE

acacacac
agagagagagag
aiaiaiaiaiaiai
amamamaman
ananana
apapapap
ararararar
asasasasas
atatatatatata
auauauauaua
awawawawawa
ayayayayayayayay
aoaoaoaoaoaoaoa
ananananananana

PEELER'S HAT

stairs stairs stairs
apples & pears apples & pe
boots boots boots boots boots
daisy roots daisy roots dais
row row row row row row ro
bull and cow bull and cow bu
road road road road road r
frog & toad frog & toad frog
money money money mon
bees and honey bees and ho
magistrate magistrate m
garden gate garden gate ga
rden gate
gar

SOSBAN

aromaaroma

bubblebubblebubblebubblebubble

aromaaroma

steamsteamsteam

stirstirstirstirstir

bubblearomabubble

stiraroma stiraromastir

sosbanbach sosban bachs
stiwstewstiwstewstiwstew
stir cyffroi stir cyffroi stircy
steak golwyth steak golwyt
onion wynwynyn onion wy
steam agerusteamagerus
aroma perarogl aromape
onion onion onion onion on

hotplate hotplate hotplatehotp

POLICEMAN

boot botasen boot botasen boot botasen
hello hello hellohellohellohellohellohello

CUP & SAUCER

cccccccccccccccccccc
cup cup cup cup cup cup cup cup
cwpan cwpan cwpan cwpan
saucer saucer saucer saucers
soser soser soser soser soser sos
cwpan ode cwpan ode cwp
cwpan a soser cwpan a sose
soser soser soser sosers
cccccccccccccc

soser saucer soser saucer soser saucer

WINDMILL

sailsa   ilsail
sailsa   capca   sailsail
sailsailcapcapcap sailsail
sai capcapcapcap sai
capcapcapca
tower tower
tower tower t
sa tower tower tow sa
sails tower tower tower sails
sailsai tower tower tower sailsai
sail tower tower tower sai
brick brick brick
tower tower tower
stonestonestonesto
brickbrickbrickbric
wallwallwallwallwall
stonestonestonestones
wallwallwallwallwallw

ARK

noahnoahnoahnoahnoa
arkarcarkarcarkarcarkar
gopherwoodgopher
savingsavingsavin
goodgoodgoodgoodgo
drowning drowning drowning drownin
badbadbadbadbadbadbadbadbadbad
cccccccccccccccccccccccc

SUNHAT

hat hat hat
sun sun sun su
hat hat hath
sun sun sun
1 shiness shiness
sun sun sun sun sun su
2 shadow shadow sh
heat heat heat heat
beat beat beat be
shadow shado
heat heat heath
beat beat beat b
shadow shadow
eat heat heat heat he
beat beat beat beat be
3 shadow shadow sha
4
wall wall wall wall wall wall wall wall

FISHES

Method: 1. Draw the outline of the fishes. 2. Make the outline pattern around each fish. Notice the difference between vv and ww. These shapes should be four p.w.h – V W.
3. Write the words inside the fish shapes.
4. Write the line at the bottom of the page. 5. Add the shape

VVVVV

6. Make the air bubbles. These are small o s – about two p.w.h.

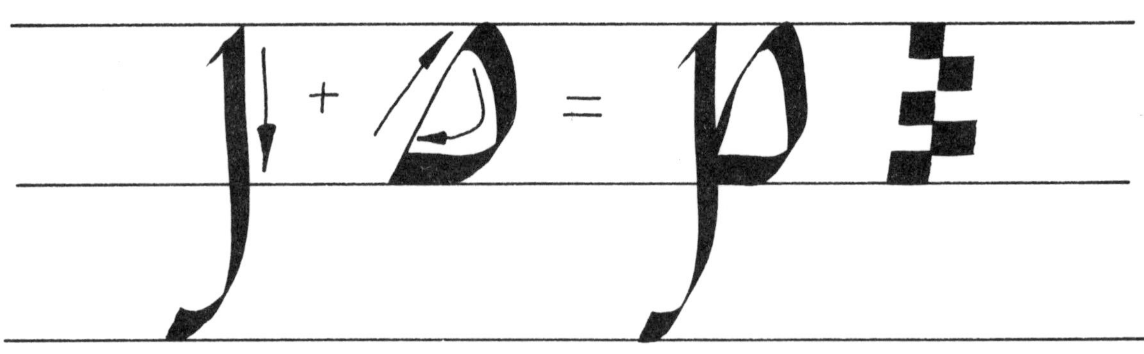

IDEAS: Reverse the positions of the fish and find some alternative words. Use a second colour for the outlines. Make another design using one shape. Put it in an oval and make it a fish on a plate. Find some more words for the outline of the plate.

seas
scalesscalesscalesscalesscalessc
seasseasseasseasseasseas
scalesscalesscalesscaless
seas·seas·seas·seas·s
scalesscales

weedweedweed
dark deep dark deep dark
sleepsleepsleepsleepsleepsleepsleepsleeps
dweedweedweedweedweed

mud and pebbles mud and sand pebbles and mud

JUG

Method: 1. Draw the outline of the jug. 2. Add the shape of the handle. 3. Make the outline pattern on the jug. Begin at 'x' and work clockwise. Notice the change in the pattern at y & z.

4. Make the handle pattern. Each vvv should be 3 p.w.h. It is easier to make these curved lines if you work from the INSIDE of the curve. This will give you more control. Remember ~ do not grip your pen tightly.

5. Do the writing inside the shape. Notice that the lines 6, 7 & 10 are more widely spaced.

The horizontal join wg occurs several times. Concentrate on the space between these two letters.

The descending letters p j g y should be carefully formed.

No pen lift is needed for the word ~ water (start; finish here & cross the 't')

IDEAS: Reverse the shape and find some different words.

waterdwfr waterdwf
jug · jwg · jug · jwg · ju
milk milk milk mi
llaeth llaeth llaeth
jwg jug jwg jug ju
clay clai clay claic
jug jwg jug jwg jug j
silver arian silver ar
jwg jug jwg jug jwg jug
china llestri te china llest
empty gwag empty gwag emp

CATS
pen lift ~ then add the cross to the 't'.

Method: 1. Draw the outline of the body. 2. Add the outline of the tail. 3. Begin the outline pattern. Make the body outline first, then add the outline of the tail. 4. Begin the words within the body.

Take care with the joins in the word

5. Complete the words inside the tail.
6. Write the two lines at the bottom.

IDEAS: Make another design using two shapes as the diagram shows.

Fill this space with text.
Use the outline only.

Look at T.S. Eliot's 'Book of Practical Cats', and find some alternative words for the second example.

cat cat
catspurrcatspurrc
catsfurcatscatsfur
catssoftcatssoftcats
catsscratchcats
cats meiowcats
cats play cats play
catsclawcatsclawcats
cats climbcatsclimbcatsc
catsand micecats andmice
catsand dogscats anddogs
cats'milk cats'milk cats'milkca
cats'cream cats'cream cats
catslick catslick catslick
catsclean catscleanca
catssit catssit cats swoosh

tailtail
swishswish
tailtailtailta
swingswin
tailtailt
curlcur
tailtai
coatc
tailt
furfu
tailt

mat mat mat mat mat mat mat mat

APPLE FALL

Method: 1. Draw the outline of the apple. 2. Draw the outline of the leaf. 3. Make the outline pattern around the apple:– thus ꝛ ooo 4. Outline the leaf as shown. ꝛ vvv

5. Complete the text. Notice the difference in spacing between lines five and six. 6. Place the words inside the leaf. 7. Add the remaining words.

Several words contain sequences of letters which do not need a pen lift.

start wonder lift

af

start wind lift

start avity lift

1 The downstroke has a STRAIGHT back.

2 The cross-stroke is made at 'a' height

IDEAS: Make a second version using two colours. Find some suitable words to fill the appleshape. An old receipe for baked apples could provide a useful text.

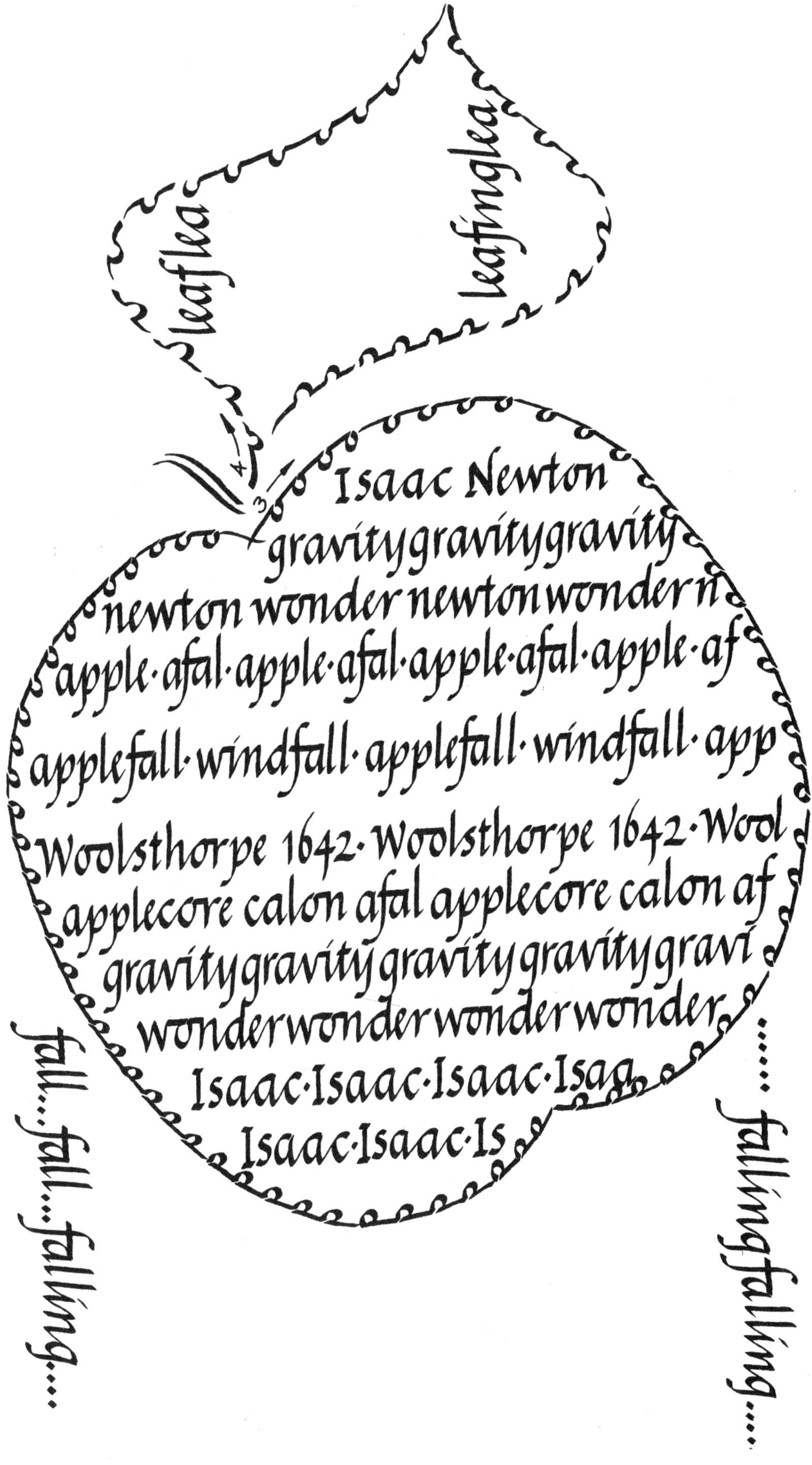
leaflea
leafinglea
Isaac Newton
gravitygravitygravity
newton wonder newtonwondern
apple·afal·apple·afal·apple·afal·apple·af
applefall·windfall·applefall·windfall·app
Woolsthorpe 1642·Woolsthorpe 1642·Wool
applecore calon afal applecore calon af
gravitygravitygravitygravitygravi
wonderwonderwonderwonder
Isaac·Isaac·Isaac·Isaa
Isaac·Isaac·Is
fall...fall...falling....
....fallingfalling....

CAR

Method: 1. Draw the outline of the car. 2. Make the outline pattern. Begin at x and work clockwise. Notice the different pattern on the wheels. 3. Make the outline of the driver's window. 4. Make the road surface and the line of words below it. 5. Complete the remaining words and take care with the spacing of the joined letters.

---

eop mog lmos

hing hop any

Try to make sure you achieve an even spacing between the letters.

IDEAS: The shape can be reversed and alternative words used. It could be made into a congratulatory card for a driving test – or otherwise!

Placed within a border it could be made into another form of greeting card – see the border designs on pages 148–51.

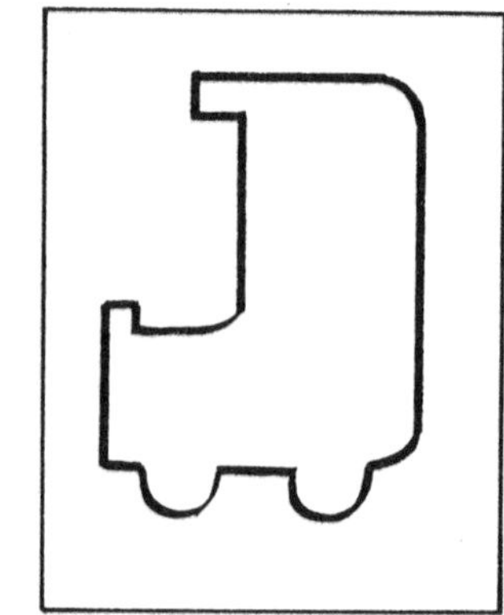

Names in CAPITALS can make useful border decorations.

cars carry people ca
rs carry dogs
cars car
ry cases c
ars carr
y moggs
cars carry boxes c
ars carry chairs ca
rs carry almost any
thing you care cars go shopping cars
go to town cars can go uphill as well a
s down cars carry brothers cars carry
aunts cars carry cargo all the way
from France

bump jolt bump jolt · bump jolt bump jolt jolt · bump

BOOMERANG

Method: 1. Draw the outline of the boomerang. 2. Make the outline pattern of vvv's four p.w.h. Start at any point around the circumference. 3. Write the text. Note: this is a condensed version, a = four p.w.h. Take particular care of letter shapes and joins. 4. Complete the lines of CAPITALS. A = five p.w.h. 5. Add the ⎽⋏⎽⋏⎽⋏⎽ decoration; ⎽⋏⎽ = two p.w.h.

A B O R I G

M N L E S ABORIGINES

Always start the letters with stroke 1. O G & S are made with a continuous stroke without a pen lift.

IDEAS: Repeat the design. Use colours for the the CAPITALS.

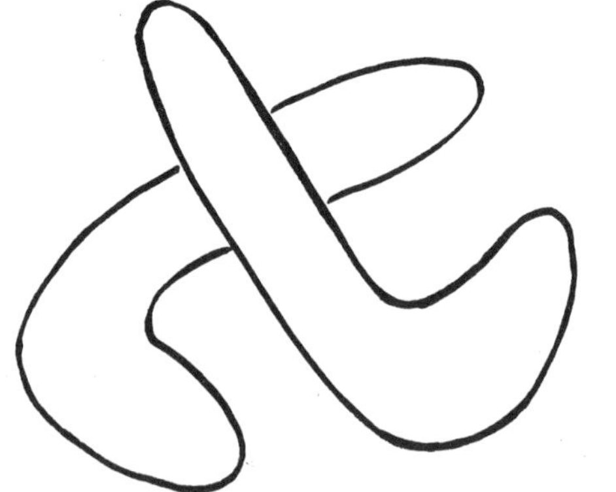

There are various boomerang shapes. Find some books about Aborigine culture and select alternative versions. Work out a design using two shapes like this diagram.

'Wisden's Almanac' – contains the names of many Australian cricketers, which could be used in a boomerang design.

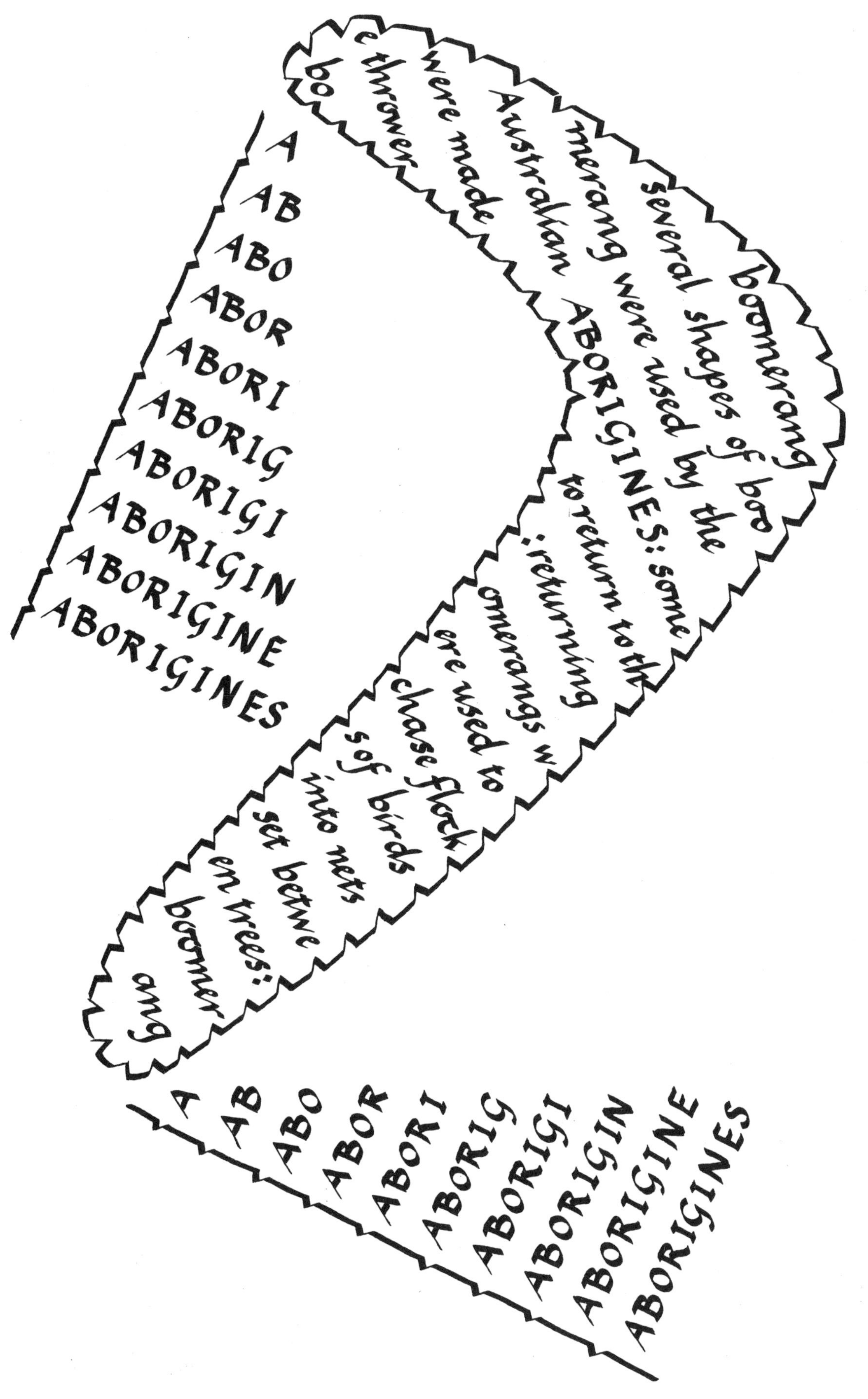
boomerang
several shapes of boo
merang were used by the
Australian ABORIGINES: some
were made to return to th
e thrower : returning
bo omerangs w
ere used to
chase flock
s of birds
into nets
set betwe
en trees: boomer
ang
A
AB
ABO
ABOR
ABORI
ABORIG
ABORIGI
ABORIGIN
ABORIGINE
ABORIGINES
A
AB
ABO
ABOR
ABORI
ABORIG
ABORIGI
ABORIGIN
ABORIGINE
ABORIGINES

WEATHERCOCK

Method: 1. Draw the outline. 2. Begin at x and, working clockwise, make the outline pattern. The vv's are about three p.w.h. Where the outline curve is sharp make breaks in the sequence thus ~ vvvvvv vv vv. This will make it easier to execute. With this design you have to rotate the paper clockwise & anticlockwise several times. Concentrate on keeping the pattern an even size. The ⁔⁔ lines on the beak are two p.w.h. 3. Complete the text ~ a = five p.w.h. 4. Add the ⌒ birds to the background, but do not make too many as this will overcrowd the sky.

---

hig her he lear home

Take particular care with the above joins.

hi he ho

DO NOT MAKE THE RISING JOINS SPIKY.

hi he ho

THERE SHOULD BE A SLIGHT CURVE AT x.

IDEAS: If you reverse the shape the words given will not 'fit' in the same way. Invent an alternative outline pattern.

Look in books or magazines for other weathervane shapes. Some look like flags, but there are many hundreds of different designs. Not all of them are suitable for a calligrapher. You need to be selective.

steeple
high near
the s ky where in sun
and rain the wea
ther cock rid
es the win d t
urning this
way and th
at h e never h
as ti me to grow
fat wit h all his twist
s and turns and yet he never
learns to crow on his tall
perch all alone ala
s he h
as no
other
home

BASIN

Method: 1. Draw the outline of the basin. 2. Decide on the position of the spoon and draw its outline. 3. Make the outline pattern around the basin ~ vv & vv = four p.w.h. 4. Make the pattern around the spoon ~ begin at x. The vv's = two p.w.h. 5. Complete the writing inside the spoon. This has two directions: ꝗ & ⊕. Write the ꝗ lines first. Then turn the paper 90° and write the lines ⊕. Fill the odd 'white' spaces with ~ strokes. 6. Write the text inside the basin. You will meet some more Welsh words here and some unfamiliar letter combinations.

These letter sequences are made without a pen lift.

laet lawd ≢ lour

candied ants ains

IDEAS: Find an alternative shape for the bowl and choose a different outline pattern. The position of the spoon can be changed. If you make it rest inside the bowl what will happen to the outlines and the words?

The basin could be made to contain a mixture of CAPITALS in different colours written with pens of different widths.

sp
oon sp
oon spo
on spoo
n spo
on s
poo
n s
spoon spoon sp
oon spoon spoo
n spoon spoon sp
oon spoon sp
oooon

currants cyrains currants cyrains cy
flour blawd flour blawd flour blawd
milk llaeth milk llaeth milk llaeth m
raisins candied peel raisins can
cynhyrfu stir cynhyrfu stir cynhy
currants currants currants cur
cyrains cyrains cyrains cy
stir stir stir stir stirs

DRAIN

Method: 1. Draw the outline of the figure. 2. Draw the shape of the drain. 3. Make the outline of the figure. Each pattern is 2p.w.h. . 4. Complete the curb line. This has two patterns of different sizes.

A
B

A is 5pwh. B is 2pwh. Try to make these lines without a pen lift. 5. Finish the outline of the drain noticing the differences in the relative sizes of the patterns. 6. Begin the words and fit them into the shape. 7. When the words are complete add extra patterns to any areas of 'white space' ~ .

IDEAS: Use the shape within a frame like the doorway shown here.

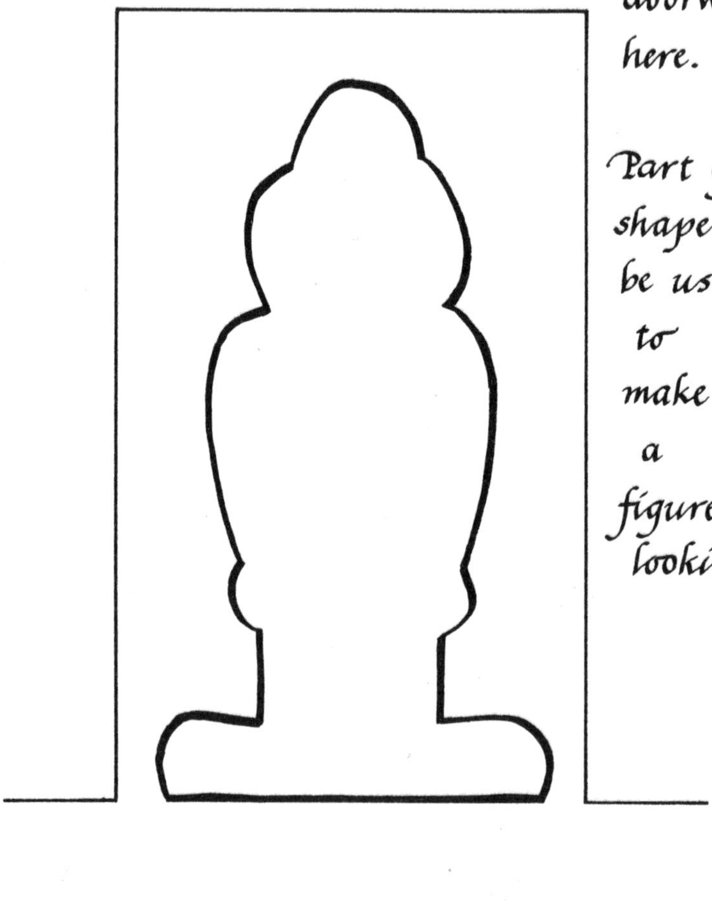

Part of the shape could be used to make a figure looking over a wall.

A small
boy stood b
y the side of t
he road. The cars
they came. The c
ars they go-ed
but the boy still st
ood by the side of the r
oad. The rain it rai
ned. The rain it go-e
d and the boy stil
l stood by t
he side of
the road.
But when I passed by
the other day the small boy
had gone away. Washed down
the drain so they do say..say..say..

TUG

Method: 1. Draw the outline of the tug. 2. Add the wavy line below. 3. Outline the area of the smoke. 4. Write the line of cccc's [y]. Notice that they are in separate groups. 5. Begin the outline of the tug. Start at 'x' and work in a clockwise direction. Most of the long strokes are slightly curved. 6. Outline the smoke. Make the vvv's about 3 p.w.h. You can vary them thus if you prefer vvvv. These joining strokes are also curved. 7. Begin the words inside the smoke. The English words are followed by their Welsh counterparts. 8. Complete the text on the tug's hull.

The letters in these sequences are written without a pen lift.

oud tur nods

mocio cwmw

Take care to avoid ascenders & descenders clashing.

IDEAS: A second version could be made using colours.
If you move the tug downwards the smoke cloud could become much larger.
Try a version with the tug facing the other way.
Find some alternative words for the design.
John Masefield's poem 'Cargoes' is a good starting point.

cloud wrap cwmwl lapic
smoke blow smociodyrnodsm
smut choke smotyntagusmutc
cloud blow cwmwl dyrnodcloud blo
cinder burn colsyn llosgicinder cols
tug turn tynnu troi tug turn ty
smoke smut smociosmotyn
eye cry crau wylo o crau
crywy low
smo
kys
chugg
chug gchuggchuggcc
waychuggbynight chug
gbydaychuggchuggchuggalonglisten
cccc to the wa vywavessing their son
song
cccccccccccccccccccccccccccccccccccccccccccc

JUNK

Method: 1. Draw the outline of the sail. 2. Draw the hull and two guide lines for the mast – 1 cm. apart. 3. Make the pattern around the sail. Begin at A and work clockwise. 4. Add the same pattern around the hull. Begin at x and work clockwise. The vv's are about five pwh. 5. Complete the mast making the vvv's three pwh. 6. Turn your paper 90° and write the text across the sail. 7. Write the text inside the hull. 8. Make the lines of ccc s in the manner shown.

12

2

ccc ccc

The ccc's are arranged in threes. When you make each letter remember that 'c' begins at two o'clock. When you make each row your pen must go round to two o'clock before you begin each reverse stroke.

IDEAS: Reverse the position of the ship. Use a colour on the sail.

A different effect can be obtained if the ccc s are arranged along a series of wavy lines.

Regular curves like these can be made with a flexicurve.

sail away sail a
way take away take
away junk sail away ta
ke away junk sail away take a
way junk sail away take away j
unk sail away take away junk sail
away take away junk sail awa
y take away junk sail away
awa awa awa awa aw

chinese sailing
ships have large sails like this one an
d they are made of bamboo~~

ccccccccccccccccccccccccccccccc
cccccccccccccccccccccccccccc
cccccccccccccccccccccccc
ccccccccccccccccccccc
ccc ccc ccc ccc ccc
ccc ccc ccc
cccccc

TOMAHAWK

Method: 1. Draw the outline. 2. Make the border around the head. The ⌄⌄⌄'s are two p.w.h. Begin at x. 3. Use the same pattern to outline the handle. Start at y. 4. Write the text as shown ~ a = four p.w.h. Take care with the spacing of unjoined letters. It is easy to leave too much space like di f er u or tor ri instead of diferu, rather than torri.

It is also easy to place letters too close together. Compare these examples ~

troed troed gwaed gwaed

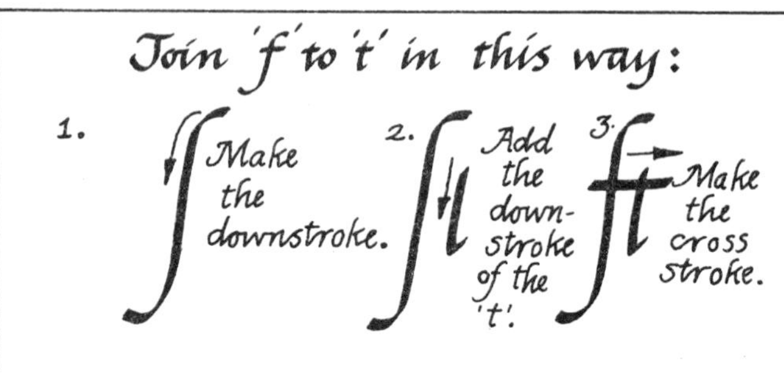

Join 'f' to 't' in this way:
1.
Make the downstroke.
2.
Add the down-stroke of the 't'.
3.
Make the cross stroke.

The letter sequences shown below can be made without pen lifts.

toma haw waed hand

IDEAS: Here are some more axes.

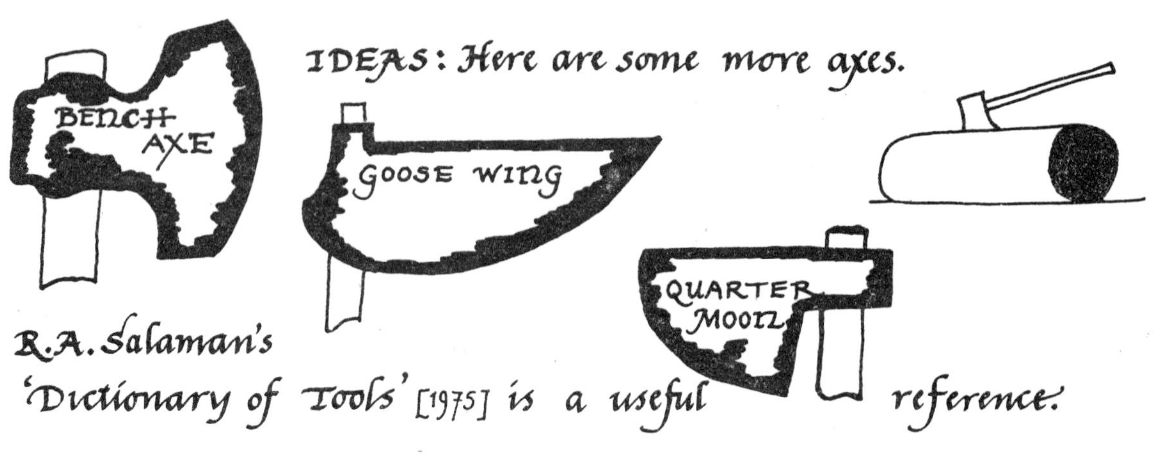

R.A. Salaman's 'Dictionary of Tools' [1975] is a useful reference.

axe
x → axe·bwyall·
chop·torri·axe·bwyall·chop·to
tomahawk·tomahack·tomaha
drip·diferu·drip·diferu·
bloo· blood·gwae
gwaed· blo
od· gw
a

y ↓
han
dle·c
oes·
haft
carn
troe
dolen
handle
coes·ha
ft·carn·
troed·do
len

·drip·drop·drip·drip·drip·drop·drip·

TEEPEE

Method: 1. Draw the outline of the teepee. 2. Begin at 'x' & write the words around the design. This text is condensed ~ a = four p.w.h. Do not leave space between the words. The object is to make a dense line of writing. When you reach 'y' make the row of vvv. Complete this line before you add the dots •••. 3. Starting at the top fill in the shape with the words and patterns. 4. Make the line of vvv's at the base; v = four p.w.h. 5. Add the capitals.

REMEMBER THE PEN LIFTS.

Start teep Lift Start hide Lift ee ee Try to make joined e's even.

IDEAS: Turn the shape around, and find some alternative words to use. Look at H.W. Longfellow's poem 'Hiawatha' and select some of his words for your own design.

Introduce some colour to your second version. Colour or CAPITALS can be useful to emphasise a particular word or phrase.

If you look at books about Indian history/crafts you can begin to work out other ideas based on the shapes of the things they used.

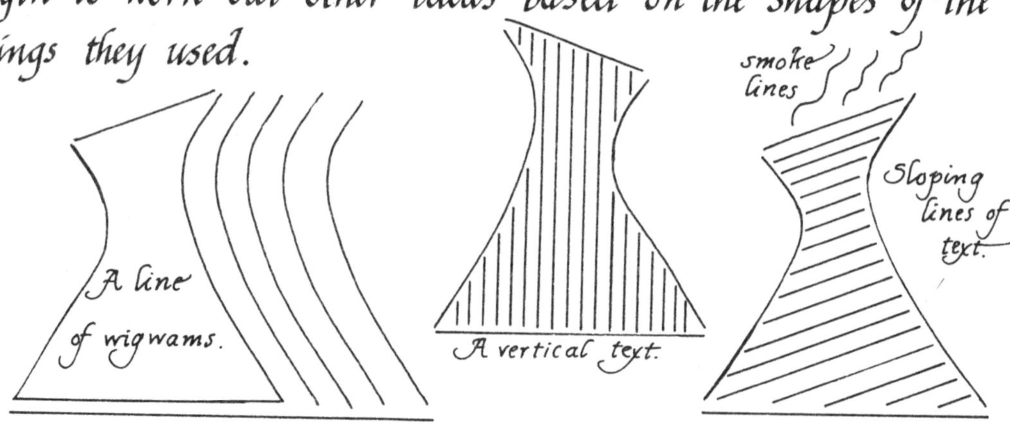

wigwam wigwam

tee

teepee tee

teepeet

teepee teepeet

teepee teepee teepe

hide hide hide hide h

teepee teepee teepee teepee te

hide inside hide inside hide in

teepee teepee teepee teepee teepee teepee

wigwam wigwam wig wam wigwam wig wam wigwam wigwam wig wam wig wam wigwam wigwam wigwam wi

·HIAWATHA·MINNEHAHA·HAION·HWA·THA·MOHAWK·DACOTA·

CANDLES

Method: 1. Draw the rectangular shape of the candle. 2. Lightly sketch the shape of the flame. 3. Make the border of the candle. The vv's are five p.w.h. 4. Write the text inside the rectangle. Notice the Welsh words with their English equivalents. There are four rows of 'acenonewoneconumon'. One version is to test your expertise in making a continuous join. The other lines are to test your letter shapes & spacing. 5. Make the two rows of vv. Notice how the vvvv lines interlock. 6. Add the two strokes to represent the wick. 7. Make the outline of the flame. These ‿‿'s are two p.w.h. Some of the joining strokes are curved.

You could add some small candles to this design. They are made with a series of pen strokes. Practise some of these strokes on a rough sheet before you set to work on the design. Start with the flame. It has two strokes & one in the middle.

Add decorations in colour.

IDEAS: Use this basic design for a Christmas card. You can find a suitable text in any of the Gospels.

Pen drawn candles can also be used for Christmas cards. Try making them in different sizes / proportions. Remember a fat candle needs a fat flame.

Allow the sides to overlap.
HOLY·HOLY...
A text could be worked into these spaces.

candlecannwyllcandleca
lightgolaulightgolaulightg
acenonewonieconumon
disgleirioshinedisgleirios
acenomewoneconiuuum
canhwyllbrencandlestic
ickerflickerflickerflame
acenonewoneconium
shine disgleirio shine di
a c e n o n e w o n e c

COTTAGE LOAF

Method: 1. Draw the outline of the loaf as the diagram shows. 2. Begin at 'x' and make the outline pattern vv & ooo. These are three p.w.h. Follow → 'a' until you get to 'y'. Notice how vv changes to ooo and back again. 3. Start again at 'x' and follow → 'b' to make the rest of the outline:~ c = three p.w.h. 4. There are 21 numbered lines. These should be written in the correct order. The minuscules (a = five p.w.h.) start at the top. Notice how the pairs of lines 11/12, 13/14, 15/16 are written back to back. 5. Capital letters begin at line four: A = four p.w.h. Notice how some capitals, in line four, are smaller than this to make them fit into the space. 6. When the body text is completed make lines 18~21. The vv's are four p.w.h.

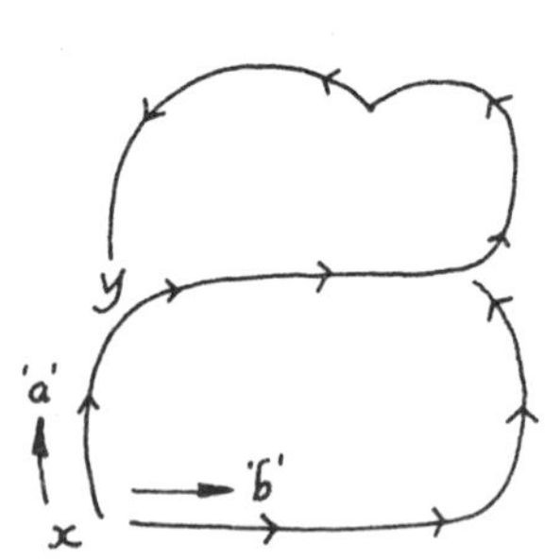

The word crust is made to 'overlap' by making the joins at an unusual place. When words are used for decoration they can often be made into a 'chain' in this way.

crust ~becomes crustcruster

C + – = G The capital G has no tail.

IDEAS: Long ago many cottages had their own bread ovens. These were domed brick structures built into an exterior wall. An alternative design could show a loaf in an oven. Clay ovens were also made in the same shape. In Cornwall they call this style of oven a CLOAM OVEN ~ cloam is an Old English word for clay. This same shape would be suitable for a recipe.

1 torthbwythyn

2. cottage loaf cottage lo aaafco

3. torthbwythyntorth bwythyntorth

9. TORTHTO·RT·HTORTHTO·RT·HTORT

8. TORTHBWYTHYNTORTHBWYTHY

7. COTTAGELOAFCOTTAGELOAFCOT

6. BWYTHYNTORTHBWYTHYNTORTHB

5. LOAFCOTTAGELOAFCOTTAGELOAF

4. TORTHBWYTHYNT RTHB

17. munch cnoi munch cnoi munch

16. cnoi munch cnoi munch cnoi myn

15. crasu bake crasu bake crasu bake crasu

14. crasu bake crasu bake crasu bake crasu

13. munch cnoi munch cnoi munch cnoi mu

12. munch cnoi munch cnoi munch cn

11. bake crasu bake crasu bake crasu bake

10. cnoi crasu cnoi crasu cnoi crasu

crustscrustscrustscrustscrustscrw

18.

19. ·GIVE·US·THIS·DAY·OUR·DAILY·BREAD·GIV

20. E·US·THIS·DAY·OUR·DAILY·BREAD·AMEN·:

21.

EGG CUP

Method: 1. Copy the outline of the design. 2. Begin at 'a' and make the pattern as far as 'b': ~vv~ & vv = three p.w.h. 3. Start at 'c' and write the text as far as 'PACE EGGING': a = three p.w.h. 4. Turn the paper around. Begin at 'b' & write the words in capitals: A = six p.w.h. 5. Starting at 'e' make the outline of the shell: a = three p.w.h. 6. Turn the paper around and complete the words inside the shell. 7. Add the letters at the base - 'd': a = four p.w.h.

In this exercise try to develop an even length for the g's & y's.

wy hogyn yolk yelk

The words inside the egg cup come from 'Old English Customs' by P.H. Ditchfield ~ 1896. Look at some other folklore books and find out more about Pace Egging. The Welsh word 'wy' means egg.

IDEAS: Compare the effect of leaving out the outline pattern as the reduced example shows. Some subjects may be more satisfactory without a pronounced border. It is all a matter of personal preference.

Try making a design using a double egg cup.

wywywy
darkness darknes
tywyllwch tywyllwchty
light light light light ligh
disgyn disgyn disgyn disg
cupcwpan cup cwpan cup cwp
eggeggeggeggeggeggeggegge
cwpan cwpan cwpan cwpanc
cupcupcupcupcupcupc
eggeggeggegg
cupcupcu
eggyegg
cwpancwp
eggyeggyeggye
cwpan cwpan cwpan cwpan cwp

An EASTER EGG is a symbol of a tomb. When the shell is broken a new life begins.

shellshellshellshellshellshellshellshellshellshellshellshellshellshellshellshellshell

mhmhmhmhmh

darknessdarknessd

tywyllwchtywyllwchtywyl

lightlightlightlightlightlight

disgyndisgyndisgyndisgyndis

e

g

YOLKYELKYOKEYELKYOLKYELKY
OLKYELKYOLKYELKYOLKYELKYOL
KYOLKYOKEYELKYOLKYOLKYELKY
ELKYOKEYELKYOLKYELKYOL

In Anglesey, North Wales, the children
go from house to house
during Easter W
eek, clapping un
til the do ori
sopened to the
m. They used t
o recite the foll
owing lines: Cla
p clap, dau wy i hog
yn bach ar y plwy. In
English this means - Cla
p, clap, give two eggs to little la
d on pa r ish. This chant was ac
companied by a wooden clapper. Th
e custom was known as PA CE EG
GING

c

d — acea ceno ncnaceno

a

AN OSMIROID MEDIUM NIB WAS USED FOR THIS EXERCISE AND FOR THOSE UP TO PAGE 81.

TEAPOT

Method: 1. Draw the outline of the teapot. 2. Begin at 'x' and make the outline pattern. The vvv's are three p.w.h.
3. Complete the text inside the shape ~ a = five p.w.h.
4. Finish the two lines at the bottom: vv = five p.w.h, a = five p.w.h. Notice that these letters have a slope (of 15°) to the right, in contrast to the upright text above.
5. Add the o's to the spout. Turn the pen to a sharper angle ~ say 60° ~ to make a compressed letter form.

To join 'o' to 't' make the σ add this horizontal stroke, then make the downstroke.

ot This is a useful join which can add speed to ordinary handwriting.

Pear-shaped, Queen Anne style teapot.

IDEAS: Find some other teapot shapes to use. Books or magazines about antiques are good starting points for your search.

Reverse the shape shown opposite and find some suitable alternative words. A list of the many types of tea could provide material for an exercise: e.g. Earl Grey, Darjeeling, Camomile, Lipton's ..... etc. CAPITALS in different colours would add interest to such a design.

x y

te te te te
tea tea tea tea tea tea
teap teap teap teap tea
teapot teapot teapot teapot t
tea tea tea tea tea tea tea tea tea
tea bot tea bot tea bot tea bot tea
capteabot capteabot capteab
te tea te tea te tea te tea te t
tea bot tea bot tea bot
tea tea tea tea tea te
eat

o
o
o
o

vvvvvvvvvvvvvvvvvvvvvvvvv

cup of tea cup of tea cup of tea cup of tea cup of

OSMIROID BROAD Va

PORCUS

Method: 1. Draw the outlines. 2. Working clockwise begin at 'x' and outline the pig; o = three p.w.h. 3. Start at 'y' and outline the base: the large V = five p.w.h, and the other vv's and vv's = three p.w.h. 4. Complete the text inside the pig. Notice how some of the words overlap: a = three p.w.h. 5. Write the text inside the box: a = three p.w.h. The CAPITALS are five p.w.h. 6. Add the grunts. 7. Provide a tail.

In this exercise concentrate on the letters p & P.

The minuscule p is made with two strokes ~ lead in stroke + = p porcus

The CAPITAL 'P' is also made with two strokes.

The down-stroke can be plain. Or it can have a side flick like this. I The second stroke can start at the top. II OR it can begin here and sweep anti-clockwise.

The reverse stroke version II can be used to provide an emphasis or fill up a white space that would otherwise look blank. A flourished P is useful at the start of a proper name. • FOR EXAMPLE •

PETER PETRUS

IDEAS: If you reverse the shape the words shown will not fit in the same way. Try this and find some other words. Use a second colour.

Find a quotation about pigs or invent some words of your own.

grunt
grunty
grunt

porcusporcinusporcusporcinusporcuspo

iggepiggepiggepiggepiggepiggepigg

apiginapokeapiginapokeapigin

porcusrexporcusrexporcusrex

Porcus the pig lived in a sty. "I know not why I stay in a sty, no not I," said Porcus the pig as he danced a jig, "but I am seldom sad and that cannot be bad."

PORCUSREXPORCUSREXPORCUSREX

PORCUSREXPORC

HORSESHOE

Method: 1. Draw the shape of the horseshoe. 2. The word around the outline makes an unbroken border. Try to make the word fit exactly without any odd letters to spare. Begin at a point on the inside of the shoe: 'a = four p.w.h. 3. Write the text on the inside of the shape. Try to fill this space with closely grouped words/letters to make a dense texture. Notice how the words are sometimes split and appear on each side of the shoe. 4. Mark out the outline of the border. 5. Place the words at the top ~ A = six p.w.h. 6. Complete the rest of the border pattern v & v = four p.w.h. 7. Add the words inside the shoe.

The Welsh words are: ffarier = farrier, hoel = nail, morthwylio = hammer, pedol = horseshoe. In this exercise the alphabet on page 17 has been used. The ascending letters d, h & l are slightly different.

'd' can be made in this way. c + l = d

c + l = d (strokes 1, 2)

At the end of a line an extra tail can be added.

l can become l (begin, lift)

h can become h (begin, lift)

(a) For speed in ordinary handwriting. The 'd' without a pen lift is still a useful letter. da

(b) od Where it is joined to a previous letter.

IDEAS: Horseshoes can be many different shapes. Find an alternative design and choose another text. Use the idea to make a greeting card.

You can find out more about horseshoes in 'Old Horseshoes' by Ivan Sparkes ~ Shire Publications.

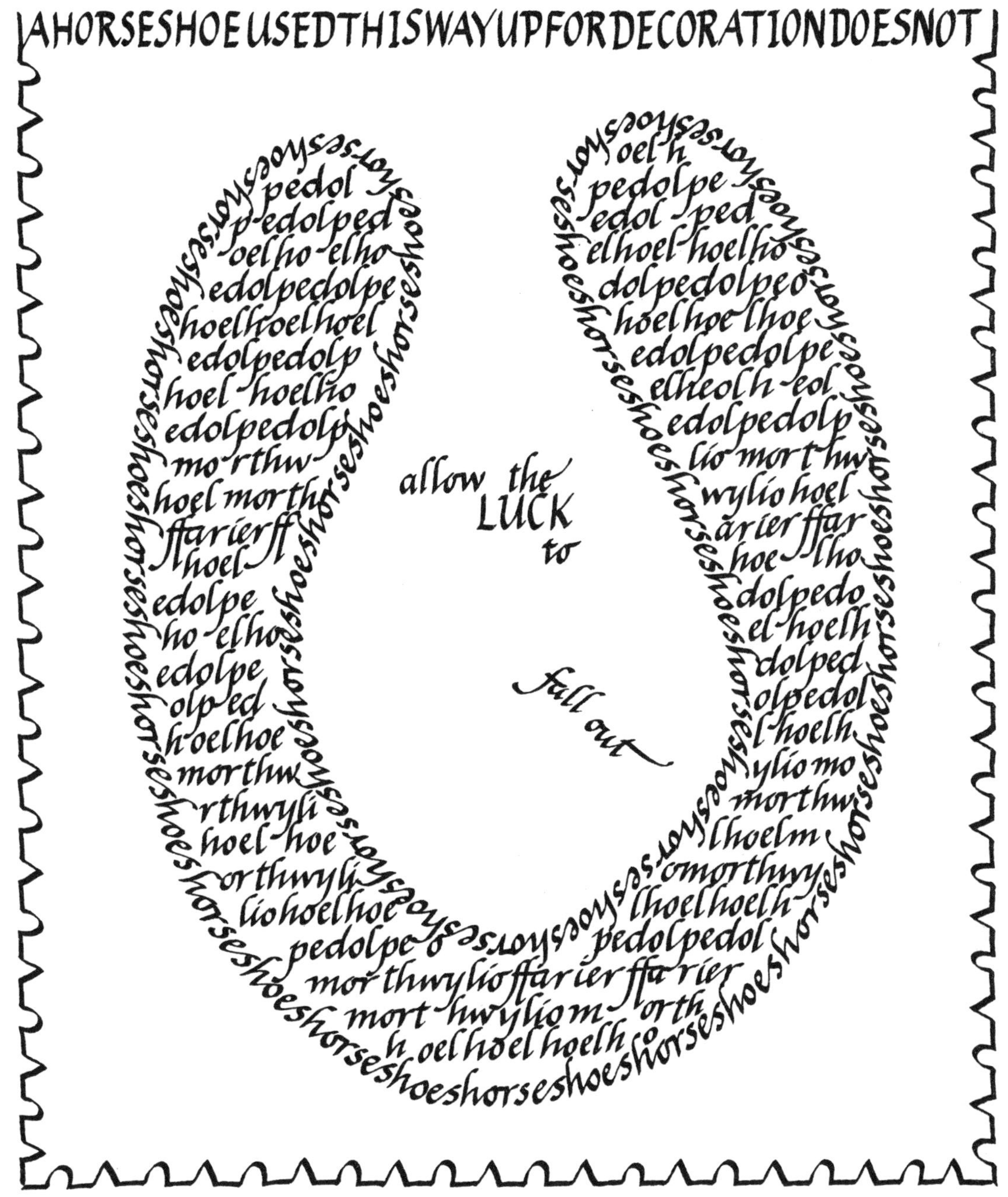
AHORSESHOE USEDTHISWAYUPFORDECORATIONDOESNOT
allow the
LUCK
to
fall out

JACK

Method: 1. Draw the outline of the jack & the shape of the inner handle. 2. Begin at 'x' and make the outline pattern vv = five p.w.h. 3. Starting at ⊕ add the vv's to the handle: v = three p.w.h. 4. Turn the paper and, beginning at π, make the ooo's (three p.w.h.) around the inner handle. 5. Begin the text, a = four p.w.h., inside the body. Leave a space between the lines of writing. 6. When the text is complete fill in the spaces between the text with the decoration ∧∧ or vvv (four p.w.h.). 7. Complete the text at the bottom: a = five p.w.h.

In this exercise take particular care with the ascending & descending strokes.

g p jack leather tman

The leather 'bombard' or 'jack' was a drinking vessel. They date from the thirteenth century and were still in use during the Victorian era. Leathercraft is a fascinating subject and a study of it can provide ideas for other designs.

IDEAS: The jack, or a line of them, provides a good shape for a potted history of an inn. The example shown here could be reversed & set inside a border. A copy of 'Yellow Pages' will supply lists of inn names. These could be rendered in capitals.

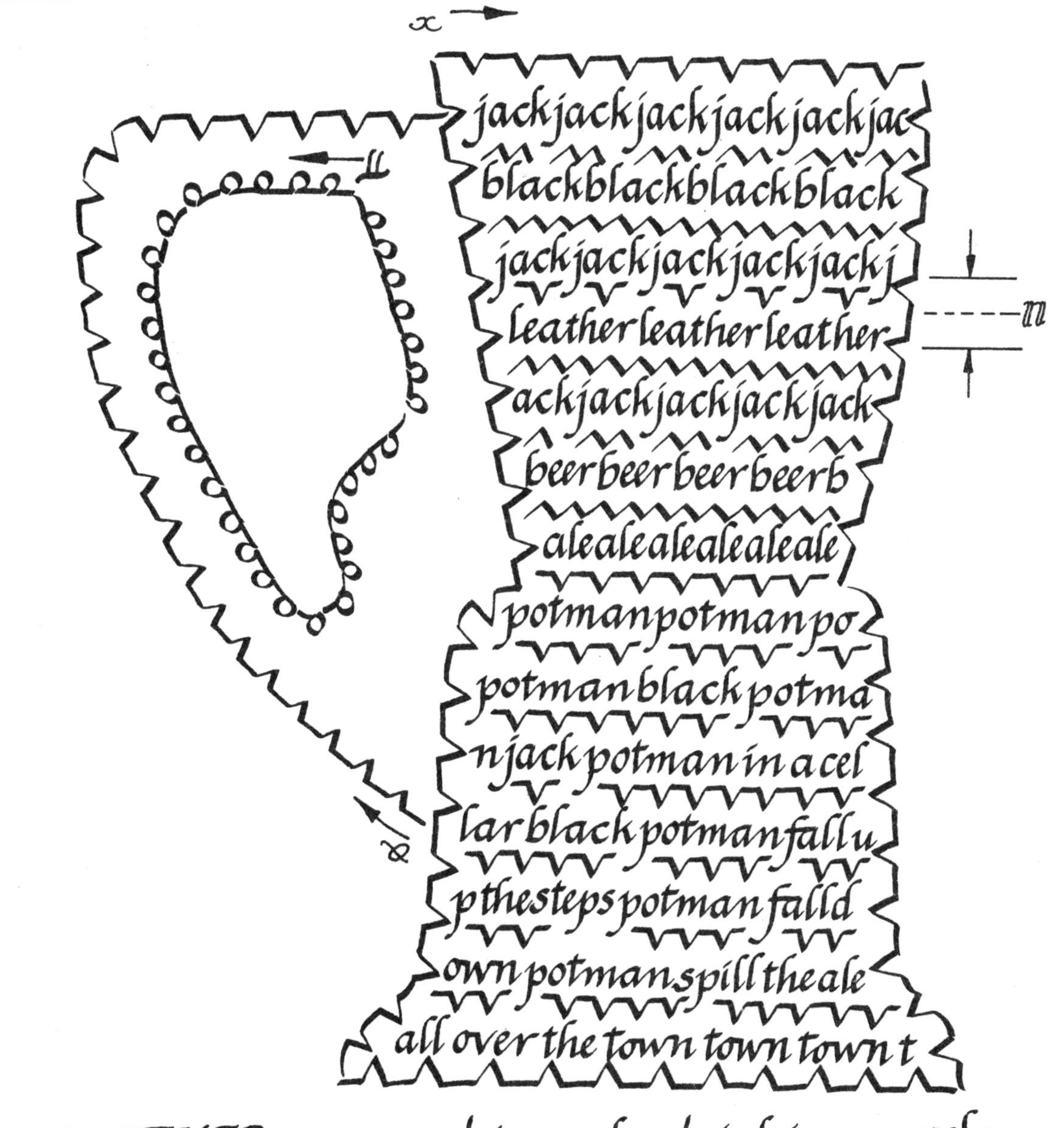
x
jackjackjackjackjackjac
blackblackblackblack
jackjackjackjackjackj
leatherleatherleather
ackjackjackjackjack
beerbeerbeerbeerb
alealealealealeale
potmanpotmanpo
potmanblackpotma
njackpotmaninacel
larblackpotmanfallu
pthestepspotmanfalld
ownpotmanspilltheale
all over the town town town t
y
m

LEATHER was used to make drinking vessels from the C13. onwards. LEATHER jacks, or bombards, were lined with tar to stop leaks.

A border could be about this size.

WHITELEAF

Method: 1. Draw the outline of the figure. 2. Begin at 'x' and make the pattern, vv = three p.w.h. 3. Draw the outline of the 'halo': a = four p.w.h. & begin the words at ϑ. 4. Begin the text inside the figure: a = four pwh. Notice the spacing between the lines. The capitals shown are six p.w.h. 5. Finish the two lines of text below the figure. One is reversed to provide a contrasting texture.

In this exercise there are several proper names which begin with a CAPITAL letter. Capitals are distinguished by their shape. They do not need to be TALLER than minuscule letters but most people make them so. Look carefully at these examples.

Whiteleaf Whiteleaf D D D

COMPARE THE DIFFERENCE BETWEEN THESE VERSIONS OF THE SAME WORD.

A small difference in HEIGHT changes SCALE.

Worcester Droitwich

CAPITALS MADE AT 't' HEIGHT LOOK MORE AT HOME WITH THEIR NEIGHBOURS.

CAPITALS MADE THE SAME HEIGHT AS MINUSCULES CAN ALSO BE EFFECTIVE

Decide on the style you prefer. Notice the w is always the same shape.

IDEAS: Landmarks can provide good material for designs. Explore your local library for topographic books. Their descriptions can supply many words for a text if you cannot invent your own.

enigma·enigma·enigma·enigma·enigma·enigma·enigma·enigma·enigm

The cross
at
Whiteleaf
is a mystery. We do not kn
ow exac
tly how
old it is.
It may ha
ve been a land
mark for the trav
ellers who came from
DROITWICH, in the co-
unty of WORCESTER when
they brought the salt: salinesalt
salinesaltsalinesaltsalinesaltsaline

The base of a chalk cliff is called the TALUS.

Whitecliff: White Light: Whiteleaf: White Cliffe:

SPANNER

Method: 1. Copy the shape of the spanner. 2. Position the outline of the nut. 3. Make the border pattern around the spanner: vv = four p.w.h. 4. Inside the spanner concentrate on the joins: a = four p.w.h. 5. Make the outline pattern around the nut. 6. Complete the lines inside the nut, and try to make a line without making a penlift. 7. Add the remaining four lines of text – a = five p.w.h. These four lines could be rendered in CAPITALS.

When you write the line nutnutnut make the continuous joins first. Add the crossings to the t's last of all. Try to make the spacing of the letters even.

nutnut AVOID nutnut

anner etter icted

A run of five letters can usually be made without a handshift.

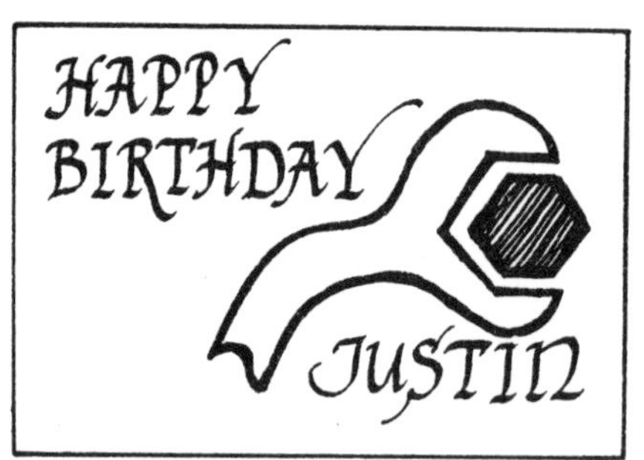

IDEAS: Find other shapes to use. Some adjustable spanners have interesting profiles. You could also try a design with a double-ended spanner.

The spanner theme can be used for a greeting card like the example shown. A decorative border, see pages 148–51, could be added to the design. Capitals can be used to make effective borders if they are CLOSELYSPACED. Colour adds another dimension but do not use too many together.

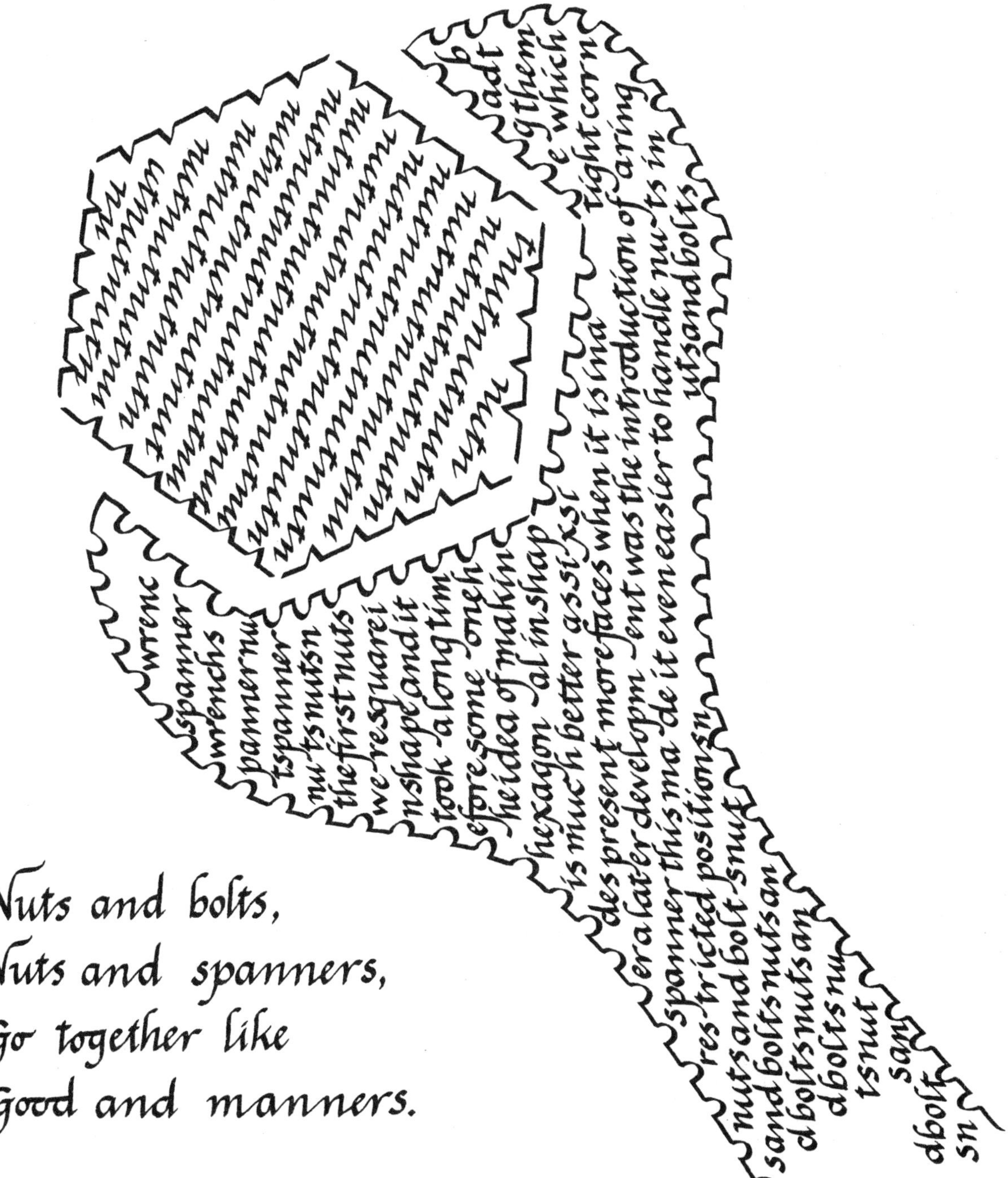

Nuts and bolts,
Nuts and spanners,
Go together like
Good and manners.

CORN DOLLY

Method: 1. Copy the shape of the bell. 2. Make the pattern around the edge; ooo = three p.w.h. 3. Inside the handle of the bell the space is filled with m & n = four p.w.h. ~ see notes below. 4. Two lines are used for the remainder of the design; both are four p.w.h. Notice how the word corncorn is made to overlap in some lines. 5. Complete the bell clapper formed from a circle of ooo's. Draw a circle for guidance.

Some of the joins on the outline are curved. Do some lines for practice before you begin.

oooooo oooo

x

'x' = Small gaps at this point can break up a dense outline.

As you work along a curve keep the pen angle constant or the letter will become flat.

nmnmr

y

'y' = If you run short of space half an 'n' will become an 'r'.

corncorncor

OVERLAPS give a line a different appearance.

ncor

This group of letters could be written alternately in different colours.

IDEAS: Draw a corn stack cockerel & find some suitable words to fill it. Corn dollies are derived from ancient symbols used by countrymen as a thanksgiving for harvest. These decorations may have their origins in ancient Egypt. Thatchers used similar emblems upon hay & corn stacks as well as cottages to ward off witches.

A thatcher's corn stack cockerel.

You can read more about corn dollies in M. Lambeth's: 'DISCOVERING CORN DOLLIES' · Shire Publications.

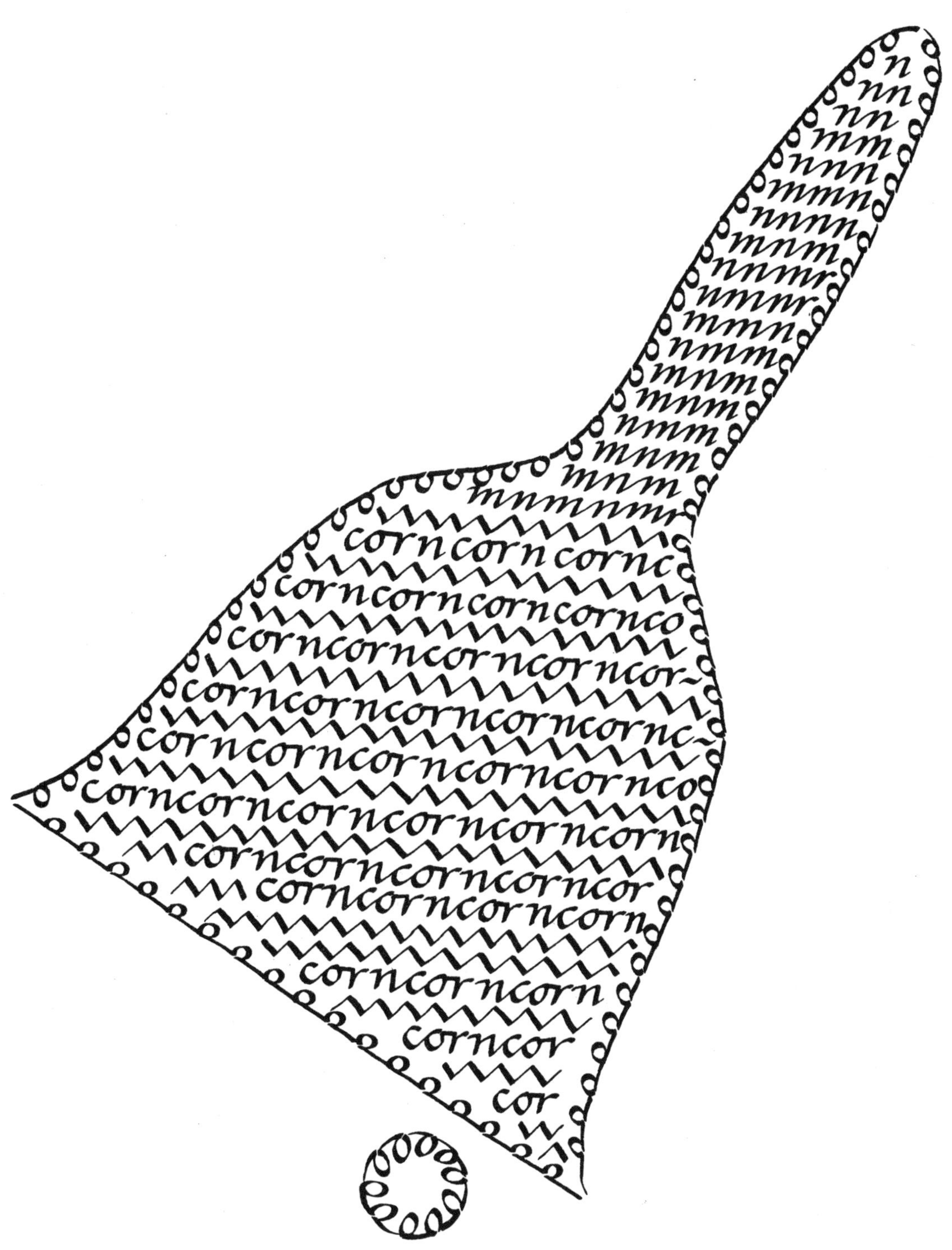

HILL CLIMB

Method: 1. Decide on the position of the road & its incline. Draw a guideline. 2. Copy the outline of the vehicle and decide the size of the driver's window. 3. Make the outline pattern around the vehicle & window: vv + wv + vvv = three p.w.h. 4. Begin the text: a = three p.w.h. This writing is condensed and you will need to concentrate on forming the letter shapes. 5. Make the pattern which indicates the road surface ~ vv = two p.w.h. 6. Write the four lines of text at the base ~ a = three p.w.h. 7. Add the brmm, brmms.

In this exercise you have to take care to avoid clashing ascenders & descenders. To achieve this you will need to leave gaps in some words.

begin

sometimes lift

This is the longest run of joins in the exercise.

& & & &

SOME ALTERNATIVE FORMS OF AMPERSAND.

IDEAS: This is another design for a greeting card. Use this outline shape to make a card for a driving test candidate. Reverse the vehicle so that it is going downhill. Compile a text to suit this change in direction.

Introduce some capital letters into your design, made with a broader nib, and use some additional colours.

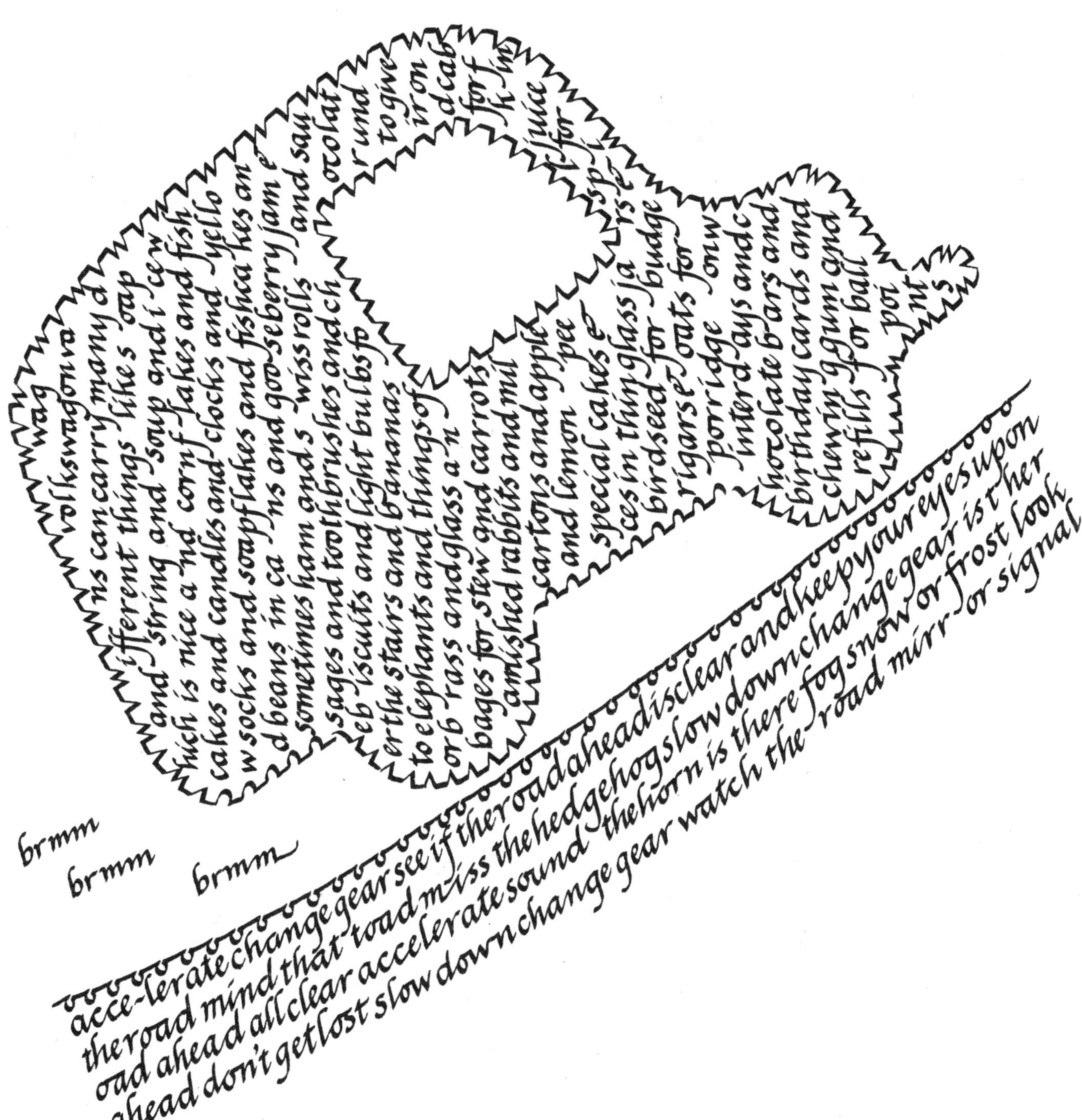
brmm
brmm
brmm
acce-lerate change gear see if the road ahead is clear and keep your eyes upon
the road mind that toad miss the hedgehog slow down change gear is ther
oad ahead all clear accelerate sound the horn is there fog snow or frost look
ahead don't get lost slow down change gear watch the road mirr-or signal

FOOTBALL

Method: 1. Draw the outline of the figure. 2. Draw the elliptical line. 3. Start at 'x' and make the outline pattern around the figure: v = three p.w.h. 4. Write the words inside the figure: a = three p.w.h. Notice the space left between the lines of words ~ see page 70 above. 5. When the text is complete add the lines of decoration as shown. Take care to 'fit' them between the ascending & descending strokes: м ꝸ v or ʌ = three p.w.h. 6. Starting at 'y' add the names around the ellipse: a = three p.w.h. Notice the absence of capitals. An alternative arrangement would be to use CAPITALS instead.

The words boot and foot have similar joins. Make them in the manner shown.

foot — lift — foot

boot is made in a similar way. boo t

ball NOT bal l

IN unjoined words watch the SPACING.

uneven space

IDEAS ~

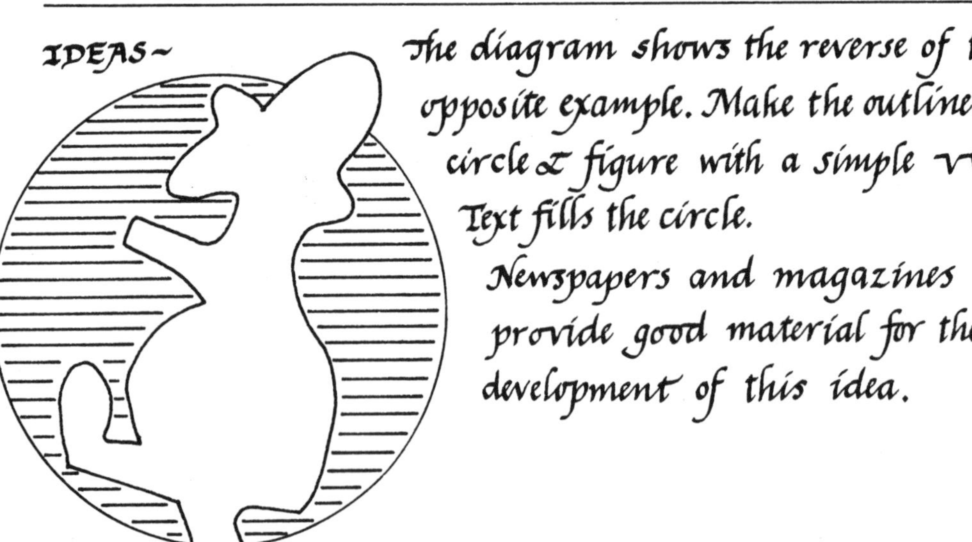

The diagram shows the reverse of the opposite example. Make the outline of the circle & figure with a simple vv pattern. Text fills the circle.

Newspapers and magazines can provide good material for the development of this idea.

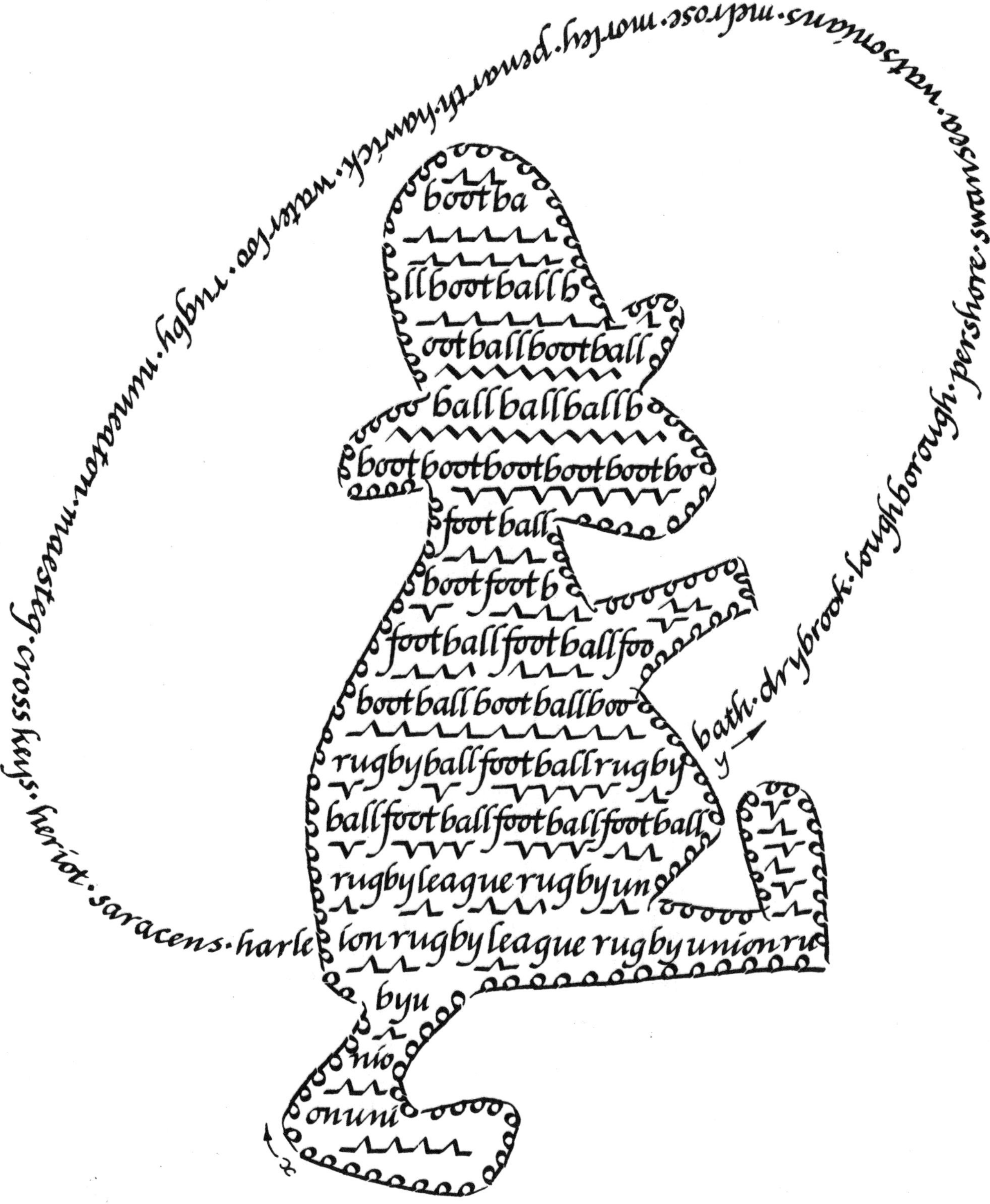
bath·drybrook·loughborough·pershore·swansea·watsonians·melrose·morley·penarth·hawick·waterloo·rugby·nuneaton·maesteg·cross keys·heriot·saracens·harle
bootba
llbootballb
ootballbootball
ballballballb
bootbootbootbootbootbo
football
bootfootb
footballfootballfoo
bootballbootballboo
rugbyballfootballrugby
ballfootballfootballfootball
rugbyleague rugbyun
ionrugbyleague rugbyunionru
byu
nio
onuni

PEBBLES

Method: 1. Draw the outline of the shore with its curved edge. 2. Draw the positions of the rolling pebbles. You may add more than those shown, but do not overcrowd the design. 3. Begin at 'x' and write the outer line of words ~ pen △ a = three p.w.h. 4. Turn the work upside down. Start at 'y' and form the second row of words. Keep a space between the lines. 5. Continue from 'z' and complete the rest of the border. 6. Using pen θ write the first ten lines of the body text. 7. The first part of line eleven is written in the same manner. 8. The capitals in line eleven are five p.w.h. θ. 9. The last two lines have taller letters ~ θ A = six p.w.h.

10. Begin 'pebble A' by making the outline ~ △ a = three p.w.h. 11. Using θ write the capitals. 12. Complete the shape by adding the smaller letters △. Try to create a dense texture, & do not leave too much white space. If you end up with a bald patch fit a suitable letter into it. 13. Repeat stages 10~12 for 'pebble B'. 14. 'Pebble C' can be formed by making the outline first: △. 15. Add the larger letters with θ.

IDEAS: The sea shore can suggest many objects which can be used as a basis of a design. Animate objects like starfish have distinctive outlines that lend themselves to calligraphic interpretation. Along the shoreline look for details ~ like a piece of driftwood. Ideas start in the imagination.

Tumble pebbles
Down the beach
Rolling, clashing
Each with each
Ever moving, never
Still: rise & fall at each
Tide's call: from CREATION until
Today you never rested in your wild
Wet world, until I came with fingers
Curled & caught you on that ebbing sea and
Took you home just for me. YOU CAME FROM SEATON
THAT ONE FROM LOOE · AND THE ONE IN THE
CORNER FROM... FROM.... TIMBUCTOO.

trickle tide sand sand ebbtide sand sand trickle tide sand sand

"PARKER 1/32" INDICATES A NIB GROUND DOWN TO THIS WIDTH. THE OSMIROID FINE ITALIC IS A SUITABLE ALTERNATIVE.

Δ	PARKER 1/32 	θ	OSMIROID MEDIUM

FISH LEAPING

Method: 1. Draw the outline of each fish. 2. Make the outline pattern around each shape ~ ʊʊ = three p.w.h. 3. Add the text to the first fish: a = four p.w.h. When you have completed the words add the dots. Take care not to overdo the dots, which could be made in a second colour. 4. Finish the second shape with a text. 5. The space between the fishes could be used for another text ~ perhaps in capitals.

The lines of writing in this design are all curved. You may find it a help to use a flexicurve to draw some guidelines before you start. It is a good idea to practise a few lines of text on a separate sheet before you begin. When you attempt work of this kind rotate the paper as you progress. DO NOT ALTER your writing posture to suit the curve!

IDEAS: Fishing can suggest a variety of ideas that can be translated into calligraphy.

The fisherman figure shown here is a simple but effective shape.

Look up some Latin names of fish to use for a text.

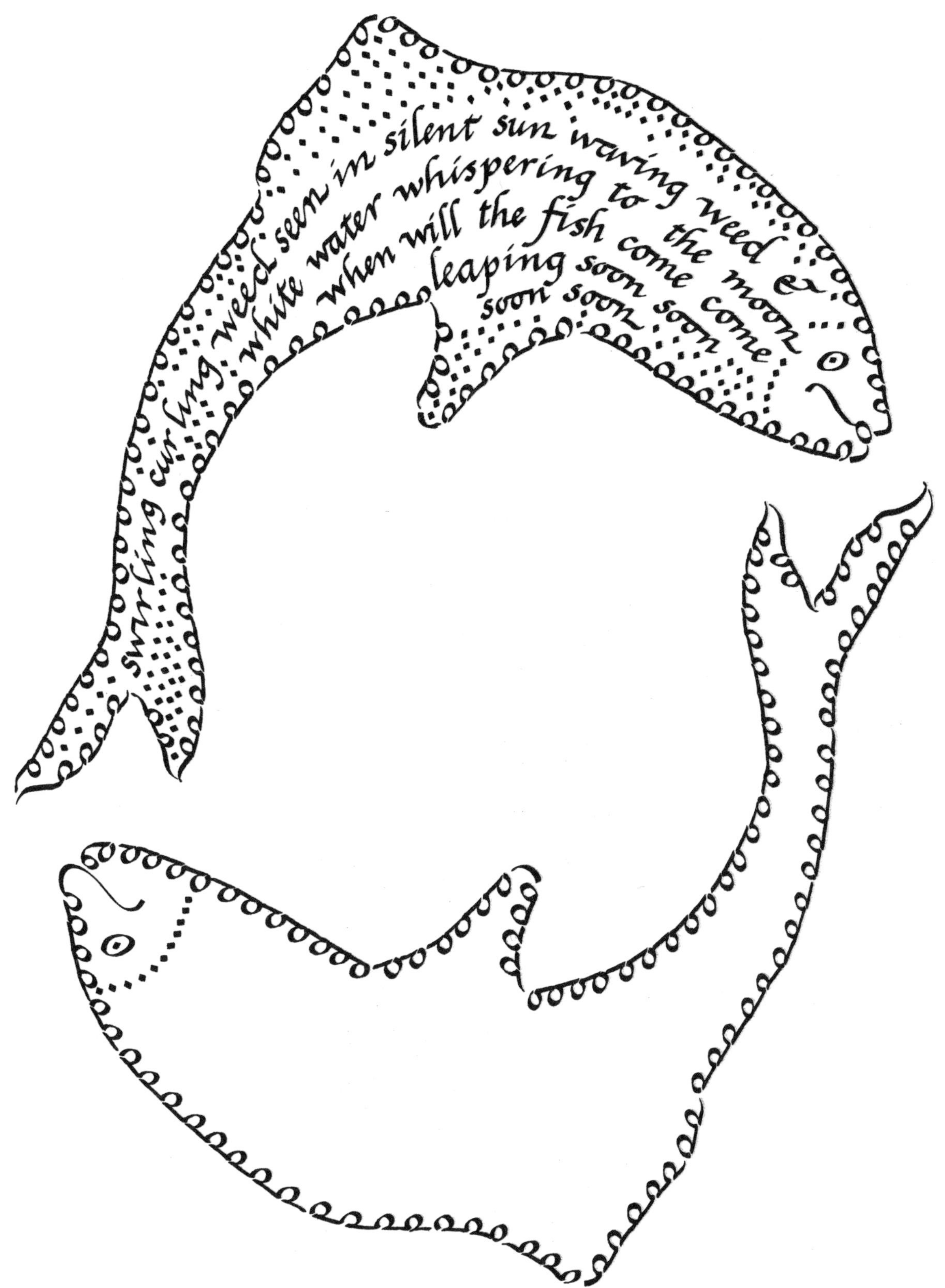

swirling curling weed seen in silent sun waving weed &
white water whispering to the moon
when will the fish come come
leaping soon soon
soon soon soon

OSMIROID MEDIUM W

HOP SCOTCH

Method: 1. Draw the outline of the grid. 2. Make the outline pattern: θ vv = three p.w.h. 3. Make the interior divisions to the grid: o = three p.w.h. ~ v = two p.w.h. 4. Use a flexicurve or a template to draw the elliptical curves. These curves could be drawn freehand. 5. Begin at 'x' and write the text around the lower curve. 6. From 'y' complete the text on the upper curve: pen θ a = three p.w.h. 7. Write the text inside the grid boxes as shown ~ θ a = three p.w.h. 8. Finish the design by making the figures in boxes 3, 4 & 5: pen Σ five p.w.h.

The figures are made with a very broad nib which makes a bold mark. Practise these numbers before you add them to your design.

7 1 2 3 4 5 6

This idea can be developed in several ways.

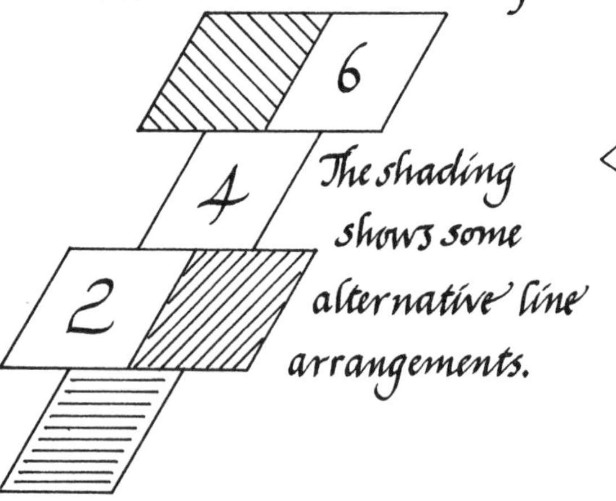

The shading shows some alternative line arrangements.

A slope in the opposite direction with an irregular surrounding curve.

skip scotch · hop a lot · scotch a lot · hop hip · hip · hop scotch · skip scotch · skip scotch · skip scotch · hip and scotch · skip and scotch · hip hop.

5

hophophophopho
sixsixsix si xsi
hophophophophop
x six si x six
hophophophopho
x six six six six

4

twotwotwotwotwo
tyantyantyantya
two two two t
tyantyantyantya
two two two tw
tyan tyan tyan tya

3

oneoneoneoneon
yanyanyanyan
on eon eon eon
yanyanyanyany
one one one one
yanyanyanyan
one one one one

hop scotch · hop a lot · scotch a lot · hop hop hop scotch · skip scotch · hop scotch · scotch skip · scotch skip · hip & scotch · hop & scotch · skip skip skip.

θ	OSMIROID MEDIUM

Σ	OSMIROID B10

TROY HORSE

Method: 1. Draw the shape of the horse and the rectangle. 2. Begin at 'x' and make the outline patterns with ⊖ ~ see below. 3. From 'z' make the inner row of ww's. 4. Start at 'y' and outline the box ~ Note the vv's are two sizes = five & three p.w.h. 5. Add the horse's mane and the grass. 6. Turn the paper upside down. Begin the text inside the horse. Use ⊖ (a = three p.w.h.) & (A = five p.w.h.). 7. With the paper the right way up begin the text inside the box. Lines one, five & six are made with Δ (A = six p.w.h.). For the remaining lines use ⊖ (a = three p.w.h.) & (A = five p.w.h.).

These strokes are used on the outline. Notice the direction of the pen movement.

Alternative versions of M. N & E.

IDEAS: Reverse the direction of the horse & find an alternative text.

Convert the horse into a rocking horse by adding rockers.

Devise a design using three colours.

·TROY·TROS·ILOS·ILIUM·TROY·TROS·
·Laomedon·Poseidon·Priam·Hercules·Laocoon
PHILOCTETES·AJAX·ULYSSES·EPERI
Heinrich·Schliemann·Heinrich·Schliemann·:
LAOCOONLAOCOONLAOCOONLAOCOON

TIMEO·DANOS·ET·DONA·FERENTES

I fear the Greeks when they bring gifts

⊖	PARKER 1/32	∆	OSMIROID BROAD

MONOLITHS

Method: 1. Draw the outline of the stone. 2. Start at 'x' and make the outline pattern: ∇v = three p.w.h. 3. Mark out a line inside this border – about 7mm from the edge.

use a blue pencil

4. Begin again at 'x' and make the line of text shown: a = three p.w.h. This line could be made in a second colour.

5. Make the remaining text inside the shape: a = three p.w.h. Take care to avoid clashing ascenders/descenders.

6. Now draw the outline of the surrounding text. The curved line is not a circle. It can be made with a 'flexicurve' or a carefully made card template. The space between the two lines equals five p.w.h. Start at θ and complete the text in capitals. You will need to take care when writing around a curved line. These capitals are written with △.

1 2 3

The E appears many times in the border. It can take several forms.

E E E

IDEAS: Look at some books about Avebury or Stonehenge. Find some more stone shapes to use for your own designs.

THE·ROLLRIGHT·STONES·IN·OXFORDSHIRE·&·WARWICKSHIRE·INCLUDE: THE·KING'S·STONE·THE·WHISPERING·KNIGHTS·THE·KING'S·MEN·AMID·OLD·BARROWS·

I·ascended·there·a·high·hill·and·travailed·all·on·the·tops·of·hills·a·pleasant·good·road·I·came·to·Rowle·Stone·where·are·many·such·great·stones·as·in·Stonidge·

Seven long strides shalt thou take & if Long Compton thou cans't see, King of England thou shalt be :~ Stick stock stone as King of England I shall be known :~ As Long Compton thou canst see not then as King of England then be forgot. Rise up stick, and stand still stone : For King of England thou shalt be none : Thou and thy men hoar stones shall be & I myself an eldern tree. Rise up hill, stand fast stone dance round the moon and call to the stars, strike frost, freeze foot, come dark come.

WORDS FROM ~ CELIA FIENNES · 1694 ·

▽	OSMIROID MEDIUM	△	OSMIROID BROAD

MARMITE

Method: 1. Draw the two shapes of the Marmite jars shown. This symmetrical shape can be made with a 'folded' template.

cut
Mark out the shape on a fold.
Cut out & trace round the outline.

You can also use a real Marmite jar. Begin at 'x' and make the outline pattern on both jars; vvv = three p.w.h. 2. Fill up the top jar first. Note the text of the first eleven lines is upright. The remaining lines have a 'slope'. Do not forget to leave a gap as shown. 3. In the second jar complete the words in the cap. 4. Turn the design upside down and start at 'y'. There are two spaces in the text. 5. Add the line of text at the side — a = three p.w.h.

In this exercise there is one word with six joined letters, & two with eight. Practise these consecutive joins before you begin.

start andwic lift — start contains lift

start vitamins lift

COMPLETE THE JOINS BEFORE YOU CROSS THE 'T'.

IDEAS: This is a useful shape for a design with its rounded proportions. Try rolling it sideways as if it is falling. Make up your own text. Bottles & jars make interesting subjects. Once you find a suitable shape think about the words which will suit it. Jars can be attractive if filled with jumbles of CAPITALS in different colours, which reveal a message. Capitals can also be rendered in various sizes. Remember jars are not always full.

x →

m · ma · mar · marm · m
armi · marmit · marm
ite · marmite j · mar
mite ja · mar mite j
ar · m armite jar · m · m
mm · mm · mn · mm · mn ·
marmite is for boys and gir
ls some with strai ghthai ran
d some with curls · mn : m · ma · mar ·
marm · marmi · marmite · marmite
j · marmite jar · marmite jar · marmi ·

toast and sandwiches toast and san
dwiches toast and sandwiches toast
toast and sandwiches toast and s
andwiches toast and sandwich
es toast and sandwiches toast
and sandwiches toast and
sandwiches toast and s
andwiches toast an

x →

marmite jar · marmit
e ja · ma rmite j · marm
ite · marmit · marmi ·
marm · mar · ma · mi

toast sandwiches and to
es and toast sandwiches and
sandwiches and toast sandwich

rt of many diets : marmite jar
land : marmite is a favour ite pa
ndwi ches in every corner of the
ite keeps its place on toast and sa
in · B12 · B2 · B1 vitamins : marm
armite contains f olic acid · niac
B12 · niacin and folic acid : m
ract · spices · vita mins B1, B2
extract · salt · vegeta ble ext
marmite contains yeast ← y

Will you do all the washing up today ? No, but ~ MARMITE.

OSMIROID MEDIUM

BALANCE

Method: 1. Draw the two shapes. 2. Use pen ϑ to make the outline vv & vv = three p.w.h. Start at 'x'. 3. Write the lines of text inside the car ~ notice the line spacing. 4. Make the rows of pattern between the lines ~ vv & o.o ~ about three p.w.h. These could be in a second colour. 5. Make the outline around the base ~ pen Δ vv = four p.w.h. Start at 'y'. 6. Add the text using Δ : a = four p.w.h.

The Welsh word cerbyd means car or chariot. Clorian indicates a pair of scales.

Take care with the following joins.

lutc fue cons ump
tion lor lance

FALSE JOINS are made by adding a finishing stroke to a letter, which is then overlapped by a stroke of the next letter.

a l can be made with a space between · BUT · al if a finishing stroke is flourished it will OVERLAP the next letter.

all is a result of a + l + l PLACED TOGETHER they become all TRY MAKING THESE OVERLAPS IN THE WORD "gallon".

DO NOT CONFUSE SUCH OVERLAPS WITH RUNNING JOINS.

IDEAS: Balance themes can make visual jokes.

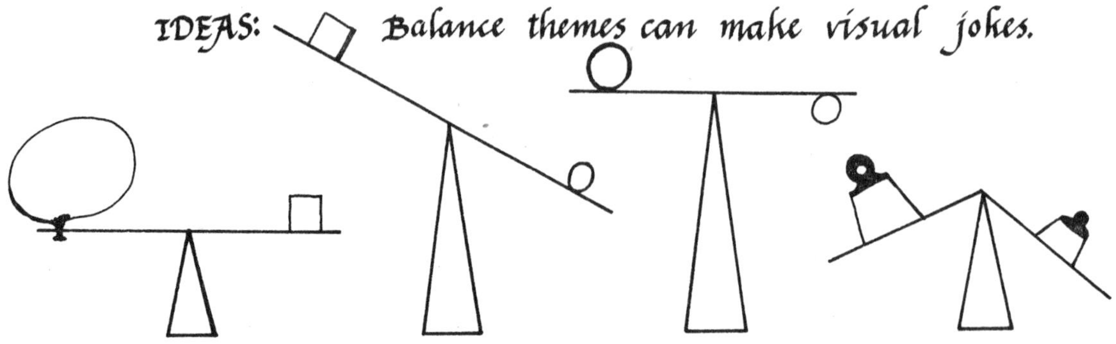

cer byd cerbyd cerby
o·o·o·o·o·o·o·o·o·o·o·o·o·o
miles per gallon miles per gallon m
o·o·o·o·o· o·o·o·o·o·o·o· o·o·o·o·o·o·o·o
fuel consumption fuel consumption fuel cons
o·o·o·o·o·o·o·o o·o·o·o·o·o o·o o·o·o·o·o·o
clutch clutch clutch clutch clutch clutch clutch
o·o·o·o·o·o·o·o·o·o·o·o·o·o·o·o·o·o·o·o·o·o·o
cerbyd cerbyd cerbyd cerbyd cerbyd cerbydce
o·o·o·o·o·o·o·o·o·o·o·o·o·o·o·o·o·o·o·o·o
miles per gallon miles pergall
o·o·o·o·o·o·o·o·o·o·o·o·o·o·o
fuel consumption
o·o·o·o·o·o·o·o
clutch clutchcl
o·o·o·o·o·o·o·o·o
miles

x

ba
balan
balance
balanceba
lancebalance
balancebalance
cloriancloriancor
ianclorianclorianc
lorianclorianclorian
clorianclorianclorianclor
ianclorianclorianclorianc

	PARKER 1/32	Δ	OSMIROID MEDIUM

SEAGULL

Method: 1. Draw the outline. 2. Make the outline pattern. Use ⊕ and make the ᐯᐯ ᐯᐯ patterns less than three p.w.h. 3. Begin the text lines at 'A' with Δ ~ a = three p.w.h. These lines rise & fall, & some letters are made to 'fit' a particular space. Before you start draw some guidelines on an underlay sheet. 4. When you reach π change pens and complete the text on the lower wing. Notice how some words are 'broken' and appear on two lines. The words written with π are condensed ~ a = three p.w.h. 5. Turn the paper around and start again at 'B': π a = three p.w.h.

On the curved lines do not join
all the pattern together.

In the text you will find several ampersands. They take less space than 'and'. Try out these versions before you begin. Use a felt pen & make them at least an inch tall.

IDEAS: Reverse the shape & find an alternative text. Try the shape given without using an outline pattern.
A 'Concordance to the Bible' will show you where to find more than 20 'eagles', 40 'birds', 3 'hawks' & 5 'sparrow' references.

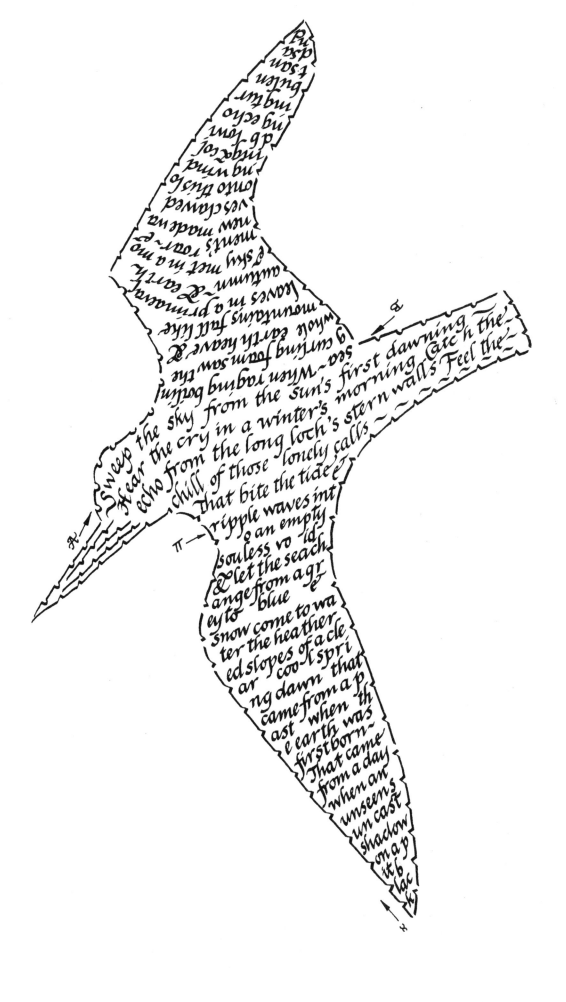

Sweep the sky from the sun's first dawning
Hear the cry in a winter's morning Catch the
echo from the long loch's stern walls Feel the~
chill of those lonely calls ~ ~ ~ ~ ~

sea~When raging boilin
g curling foam saw the
whole earth heave &
mountains fall like
leaves in a primaeval
autumn~& earth
& sky met in a mo
ment's roar~&
new made wa
ves clawed
onto this lo
ng wind
ing & col
d b lowi
ng echo
ing tur
bulen
t san
dsa
Pu

That bite the tide e
ripple waves int
o an empty
souless vo id
& let the seach
ange from a gr
ey to blue e
snow come to wa
ter the heather
ed slopes of a cle
ar cool spri
ng dawn that
came from a p
ast when th
e earth was
first born~
That came
from a day
when an
unseen s
un cast
shadow
on a p
it b
lac
k

ϑ	PARKER 1/32	Δ	CROSS SI	π	OSMIROID MEDIUM

OUCH

Method: 1. Draw the outline of the two shapes. 2. With pen ϑ make the outline patterns σσ - vv - vvv = three p.w.h. Start at 'x' & 'y'. 3. Start the text (pen Δ) in the axe head: a = three p.w.h. Notice the way in which the word axe iron 'overlaps'. Take care with the word haft and 'fit' it carefully into the handle. 4. Write the text inside the block. Finish the words first: a = three p.w.h. Then add the decorations vv & w. 5. With pen β write the OUCH which should be about six p.w.h.

Another example of an overlapping word.

Alternative versions.

axeironaxeiron x x x

Practise before you start.

vineous sanguine

Take care with the running joins.

IDEAS: This subject may remind the reader of castles and dungeons. Barred doors or the outlines of old village lock-ups can make interesting designs.

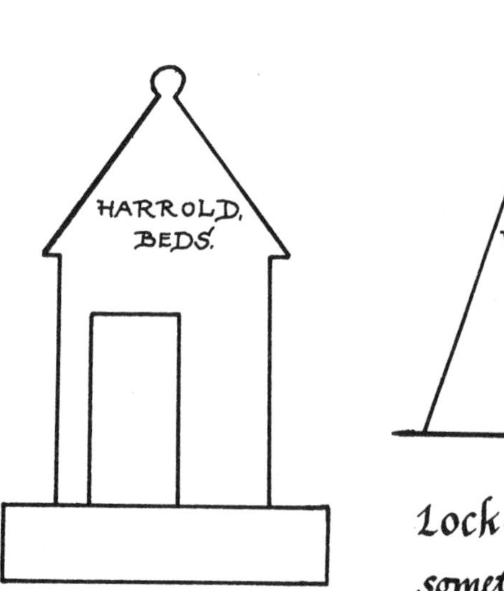

Lock-ups were often windowless. They are sometimes called blind houses.

θ	BARKER 1/32	Δ	CROSS SI	β	SHEAFFER MED.

MITRE

Method: 1. Draw the mitre shape and the two curved 'labels' below it. 2. Use ⊖ to make the outline pattern, starting at 'x': oo & vv = three p.w.h. 3. Make the upper line of the label start at 'A' & 'B' ~ oo = three p.w.h. 4. Turn the paper upside down & start the vv pattern at 'C' & 'D'. The vv's = four p.w.h. ~ see note below. 5. Begin the text inside the mitre. Write all the 'sanctus' lines first ~ ⊖ a = four p.w.h. 6. Reverse the paper and begin the 'sanctaidd' lines. These are written on the other side of the 'sanctus' line ~ leave a small space between the two rows of words. A second colour could be used. 7. Begin at 'E' and make the outline of the rectangle ~ draw some guide lines first. Pen Δ vv = six p.w.h. 8. Write the text inside this space ~ a = five p.w.h. Notice that the letters are unjoined. Take care with the figures.

WATCH THE SPACES BETWEEN THO THE oo'S. IF IT IS TOO SMALL THE vv'S WILL NOT FIT IN.

Try to write these letters without a pen lift.

START
sanctaidd
LIFT

IDEAS: Use this outline and invent an alternative text ~ an invitation to a church event.

The mitre shape on its own could be used for a greeting card. Try setting the mitre inside a square border.

sanc
tus · sanc
tus · sanctus ·
sanctus · sanctus · san
ctus · sanctus · sanctus · san
ctus · sanctus · sanctus · sanct
us · sanctus · sanctus · sanctus
sanctus · sanctus · sanctus · s
anctus · sanctus · sanctus
sanctus · sanctus · sanc
tus · sanctus · sanctus
sanctus · sanctus ·
sanctus · sanctus
sa nct

A B C D E K

Bishops of the West Saxons & WINCHESTER ~:~:~:~
634 Birinus ~ 650 Aegilbert ~ 662 Wine ~ 670 Eleu-
therius ~ 676 Haeddi ~ 705 Daniel ~ 744 Hunferth ~

⊖	Parker 1/32	Δ	Osmiroid medium

SPIRALS

Method: These two diagrams show you how to make spirals.

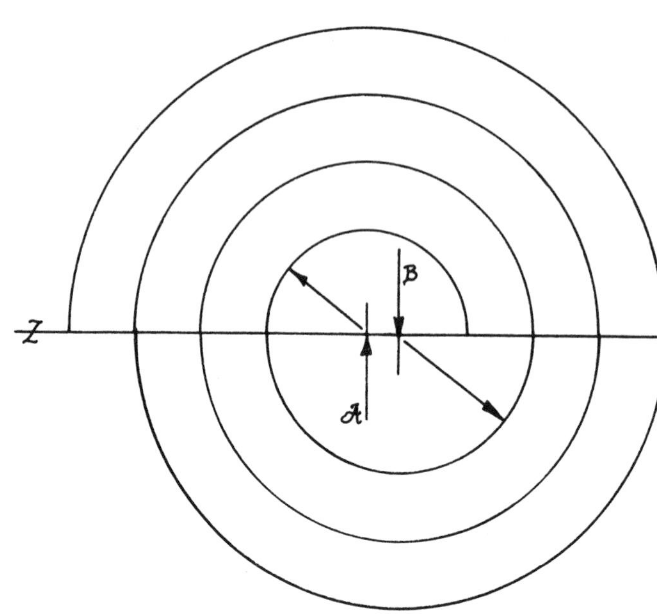

ANTICLOCKWISE

1. Draw the line Z~Z.
2. Mark centres A & B~ spaced 5mm. apart.
3. From A make semi-circles with radii of 2½ cm., 3½ cm., 4½ cm., & 5½ cm. etc.
4. From B make semi-circles with radii of 2cm., 3cm., 4cm., 5cm. etc.

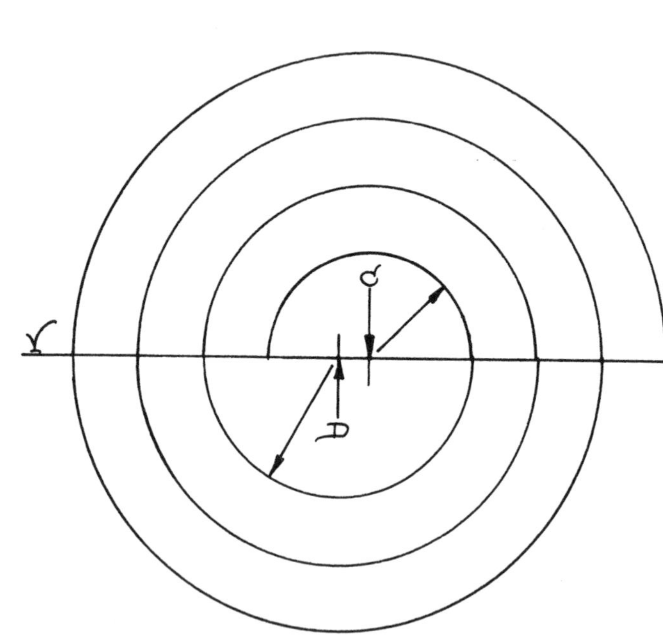

CLOCKWISE

1. Draw the line Y~Y.
2. Mark centres C & D~ spaced 5mm. apart.
3. From C make semi-circles with radii of 2½ cm., 3½ cm., 4½ cm., & 5½ cm. etc.
4. From D make semi-circles with radii of 2cm., 3cm., 4cm., 5cm. etc.

When you write around a spiral all the ascending or descending strokes should point to the centre. This is not easy to do when you are constantly rotating the paper. REMEMBER ~ Do not change your posture to suit the curve!

From the top of this high land called 'Morning Hill', & the real name of which is 'Magdalen Hill', from a chapel which once stood there dedicated to MARY MAGDALEN; from the top of this land you have a view of a circle which is upon average about seventy miles in diameter; & I believe in no one place so little as fifty miles in diameter. You see the isle of Wight in one direction, and in the opposite you see the high lands in Berkshire. Descending from this hill you cross the turnpike road leading from Winchester to Alresford.

WORDS FROM~
WILLIAM COBBETT'S
'RURAL RIDES'.

	OSMIROID MEDIUM W

AGNUS DEI

This design is based upon a double spiral. To make guidelines use a paper with 5mm. squares.

Method: 1. Draw a centre line C–C. 2. Draw, with a soft pencil, the central 1 CM. square.

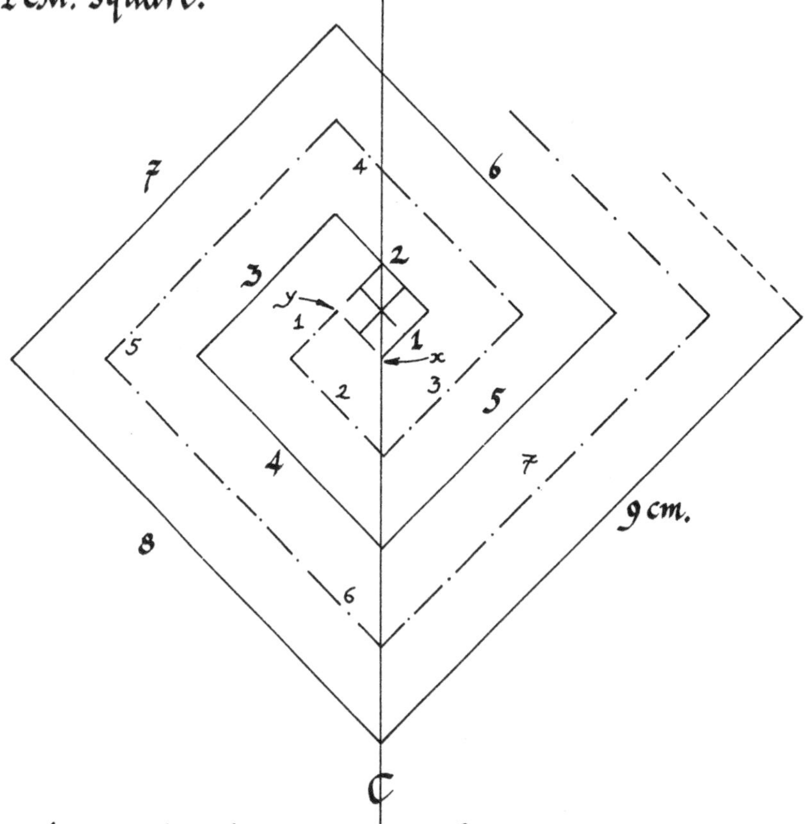

3. Start at 'x' & make the sequence of lines shown: 1, 2, 3, 4, 5, 6, 7 cms long. 4. Start at 'y' and make the second set of lines —·—·— 1, 2, 3, 4, 5, 6 cms etc. 5. Begin at 'x' & write the text "O Lamb of God....". 6. When the sequence is complete start at 'y' and write the "Agnus Dei... " text.

IDEAS: Use different colours for lines 'x' & 'y'. Make one line in capitals.

Agnus Dei, qui tollis peccata mundi, dona eis requiem. Lux aeterna luceat eis, Domine cum sanctis tuis in aeternum, qui pius es. Requiem aeternam dona eis, Domine, et lux perpetua luceat eis. Dona eis requiem. Dona eis requiem sempiternam.

O Lamb of God, who takes away the sins of the world, give them rest. Let light perpetual shine upon them together with thy saints for thou art good. Eternal rest grant unto them, O Lord, and let perpetual light shine upon them. Grant them eternal rest. Dona eis; Dona eis requiem.

	OSMIROID BROAD W

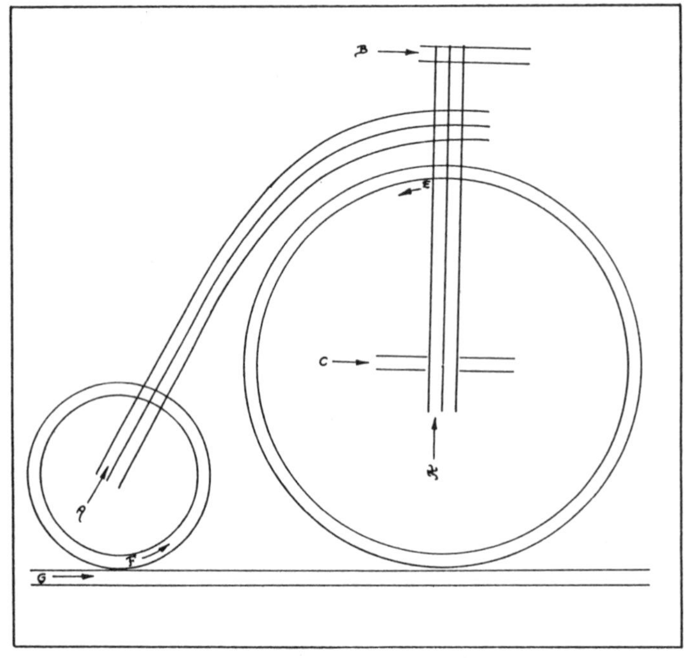

PENNY FARTHING

Method. 1. Use a compass & draw the two pairs of circles. The space between the lines will fix the size of the letters. 2. Draw the guidelines A to G. 3. Begin at A & write the sequence acea..etc. Try to avoid pen lifts. At the end of the line reverse the paper & make the second line of double text. 4. Make lines B & C. 5. Start at D & make the upper line of text. Reverse the paper to complete the line. 6. From E begin the big wheel. 7. Repeat the process for F. 8. Make the ground line G.

Ideas: Reverse the shape. Add colours. Devise an alternative text or patterns. Add a rectangular border.

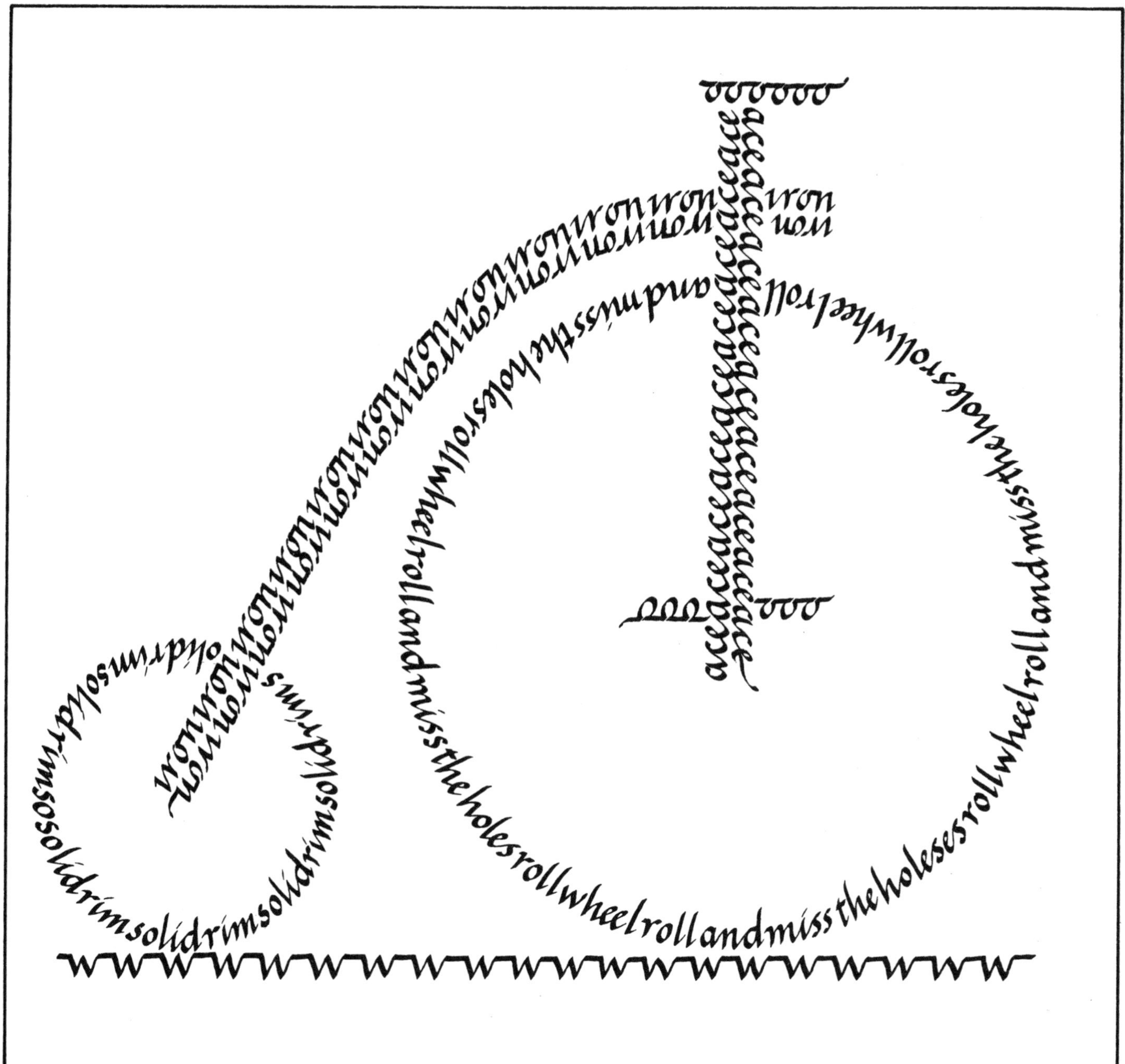

OSMIROID MEDIUM

ELMS

Method: 1. Draw the outline of the tree. 2. Make the outline pattern: ∪∪–& ooo = three p.w.h. Begin at 'x'. 3. Start the text inside the tree. Notice the reversed lines at 'y'. 4. Add the text at the base & use the ~ decorations to fill the spaces. (a = three p.w.h.) (A = five p.w.h.).

This letter sequence appears frequently. Practise it on a separate sheet before you start.

ulmus

NO PEN LIFT

Leaf forms can be made with two strokes.

IDEAS: Change the position of the tree & use two different greens for the foliage.

The text at the base could be placed within a border.

More ideas about elms can be gleaned from Gerald Wilkinson's splendid 'Epitaph for the Elm' ~ 1978.

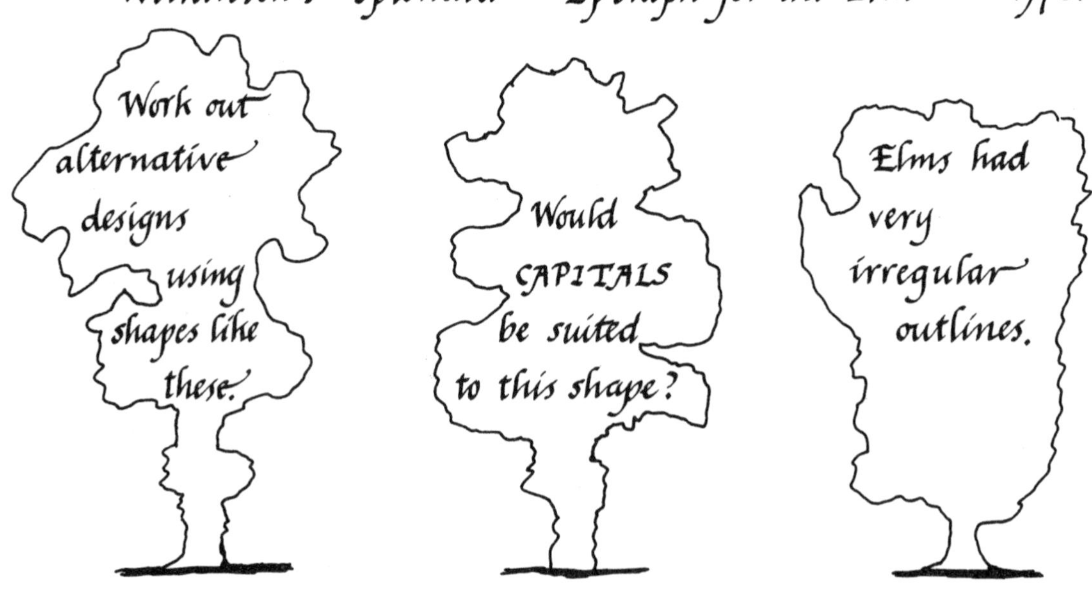
Work out alternative designs using shapes like these.
Would CAPITALS be suited to this shape?
Elms had very irregular outlines.

umus
Ulmus Ulmus
procera procera pr
is the English Elm
Ulmus americana is t
he American White Elm
Ulmus laevis is the E
uropean White Elm
Ul-mus glabra is the
Wych Elm Ulmu
s carpinifolia is
the Sm-ooth Leafe
d Elm Ulmus holla-n
dica is the Dutch Elm Ulm
us pumila is the Siberian E
l-m ~ ulmus ulmus ulmus ulm
Ulmus parvifolia is the Chines
e Elm ulm-us ulmus ulmusu
Ulmus Wheatleyi is the Wheatl
ey Elm ulmus ulmus ulmus ul
ulmus ulmus ulmus ulmus ulmu
ulmus ul musul musu
ulmu
ulmu
ulmus
ulmusu
lmusulmu
sulmus ulmusu

The English Elm which once stood along the hedgerows has now al-most disappeared. It has been destroyed by the fungus CERATOCYSTI-S ULMI carried by the bark-beet-le SCOLYTUS-SCOLYTUS. More than eleven million trees have been lost.

AKU AKU

These two examples derive from Thor Heyerdahl's writings. Make the outline pattern first and then arrange the text. The Polynesian words are: Rapi Nui = Easter Island; hani hani = porridge; rongo rongo = symbolic writing; hanu eepe = long ears; kumara = sweet potato; 1 = etahi; 2 = erua; mamama nuihi = dolphin.

The outline pattern is made with a simple downstroke. Notice how changing the slope angle alters the width.

In the border an alternative version of A is shown.

Increasing the angle narrows the letter.

WATCH THE PROPORTIONS OF THIS SPACE.

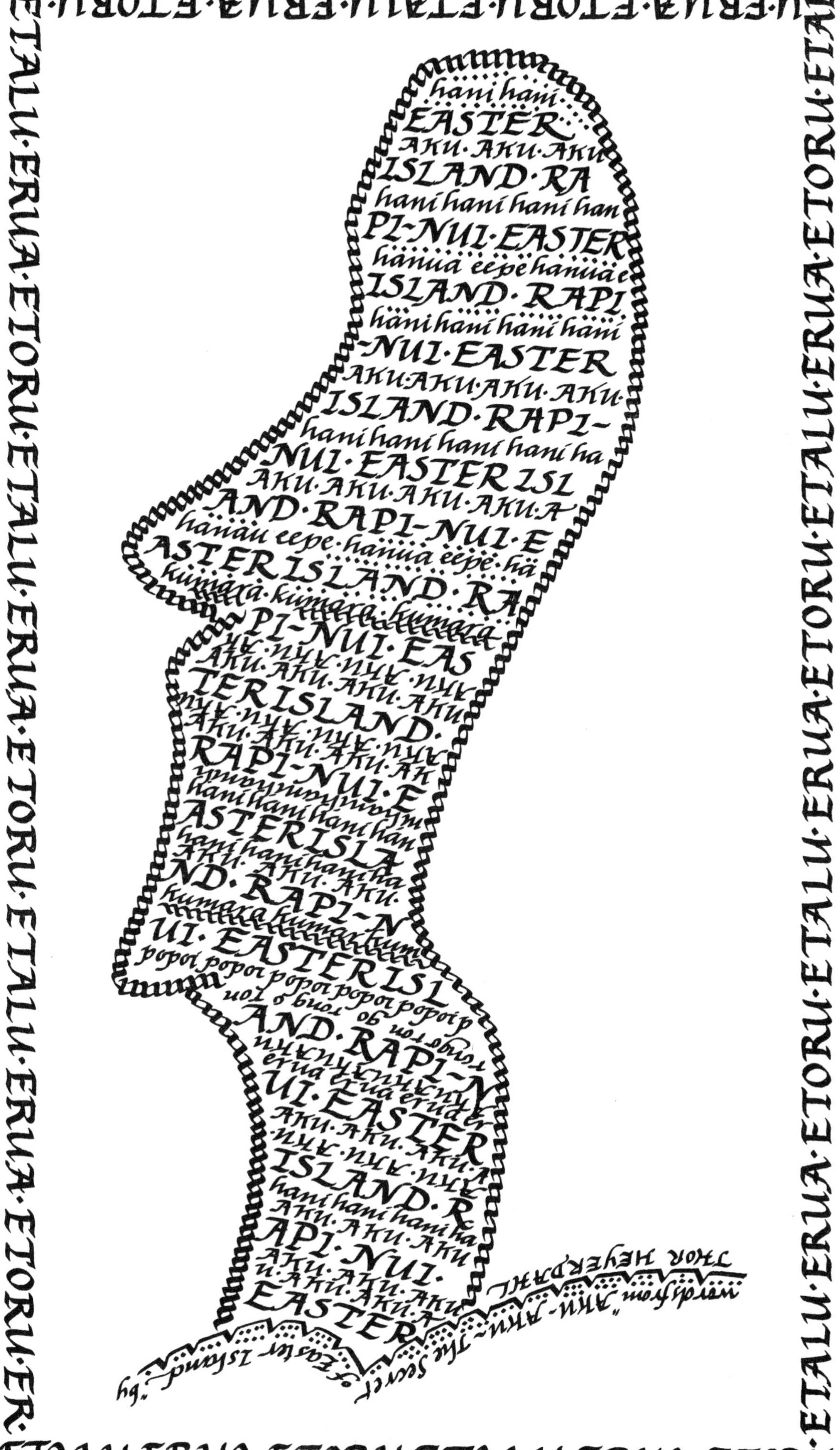

	PARKER 1/32 ⋀⋀⋀⋀		OSMIROLD BROAD ⋁⋁

STONEHENGE

Method: 1. Draw the outline of the trilithon. 2. Begin at 'x' & make the outline pattern vv = three p.w.h. 3. Start at 'y' & complete the vv = three p.w.h. 4. The text inside the shape, a = three p.w.h., is closely spaced. Avoid clashing ascenders/descenders. Notice the line of capitals. Some words appear partly on each upright ~ e.g. 'sols — tice'. 5. The line of capitals at the base is five p.w.h. 6. Complete the remaining text: a = three p.w.h. & the capitals are four p.w.h. The capitals could be rendered in a second colour.

---

lintelintelintelintelintelin

These letters are arranged in a way which makes each letter 'l' part of two words. By overlapping words in this fashion the rhythm of the writing is changed.

IDEAS: Standing stones always have an air of mystery. Their distinctive shapes can provide a framework for many designs.

The design shown here could be set within a rectangular border. Capitals closely spaced can make effective borders.

See also ~ page 148.

Stonehenge Stone
heelstone he elstone heelston
cursuscursus cursuscursus cursuscurs u s
lintelintelintelintelintelintelintelintelintelintelint
trilithon trilithon trilithon trilithon trilithon trilitho
mortice & tenon mortise & tenon mortice & tenon m
bluestones bluestones bluestones bluestones b
monument monument monu

DRUIDRU IDRUIDRU
summers ummers
solsticesols ticesolstic
sarcenssar censsars
AubreyAub reyAubr
horse shoeh orseshoe
altarstonea ltarsto
earthworks earthw
vallumvallu mvallu
fossefossefos sefossefo
sun sun su sun su
axsisaxsisa xsisaxsis
symbolisms ymbolis
bronze bron zebronz
stonesstones stonesston
circlecirclec ircle circle
cursuscurcu rsuscurs
heelheelheelhe lehelehelehe

·LATE NEOLITHIC·EARLY BRONZE·AGE·

The first BARONET CHUBB presented the unique site of STONEHENGE to the nation. This ancient monument appears on the arms of CHUBB. The background of the Chubb shield is blue & green ~ sky & grass. The trilithon is white.

OSMIROID MEDIUM N

CAR PARK

Method: 1. Draw the outline of one vehicle on a thin sheet of card. 2. Cut out this shape. 3. Place the shape on the paper & draw a line around it. 4. Use the shape to fill up the remainder of the space in the way shown opposite. 5. On each car in turn (a) make the outline pattern : a, vv, vv etc. = three p.w.h. (b) make the outline of the window. 6. Complete the text inside each vehicle. It is best to finish one vehicle at a time.

The letter x shown in this exercise has an extended downstroke thus:

1 λ + 2 ſ = x

The word

waiting

is written without a pen lift.

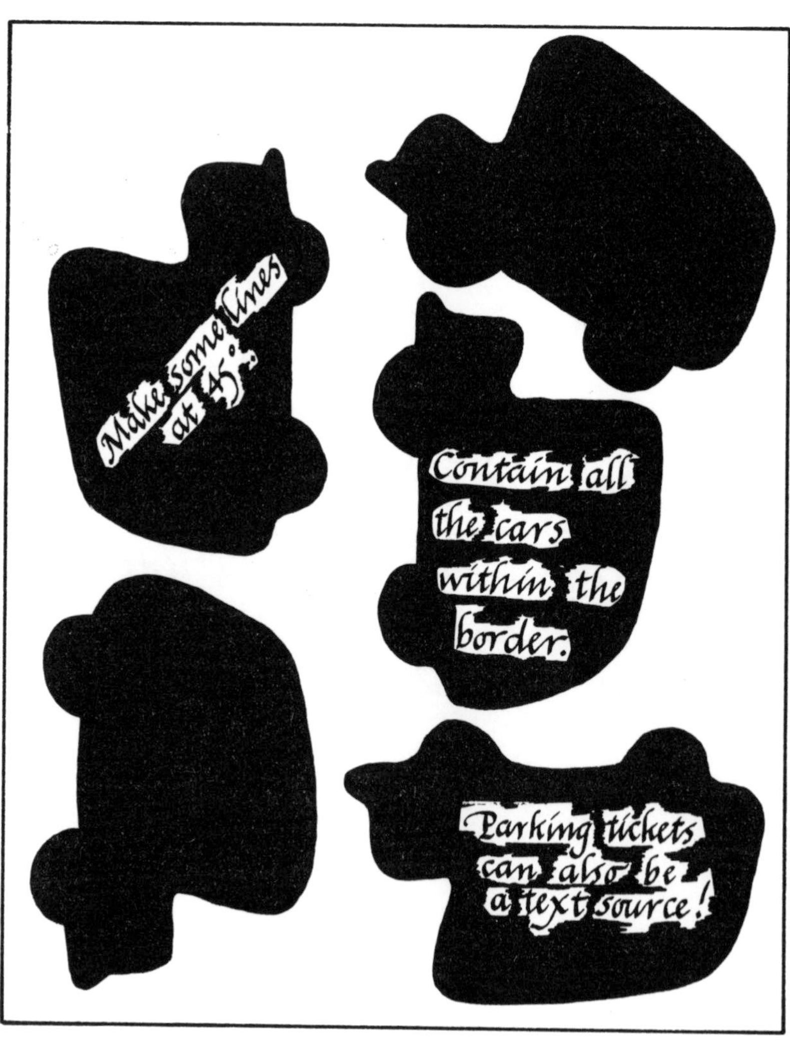

IDEAS

Rearrange the cars and introduce a second car shape. An alternative text can be compiled from car names, racing drivers or car spares. A border could be made to surround your car park.

CAR
PARK

ticket ticket ticket ticket
ma chine ma
bar rier barrie
no change no
res erve drese
dis abled disab
driv ers only only
no reverse no reverse no reversen
no waiting no waiting no waiting no wai
exit exit exit exit exit exit exit exit exit exit
no entry no entry no entry no entry no
stop stop stop stop stops to
spaces spaces s
room room
ma

EXIT

PARKER 1/32

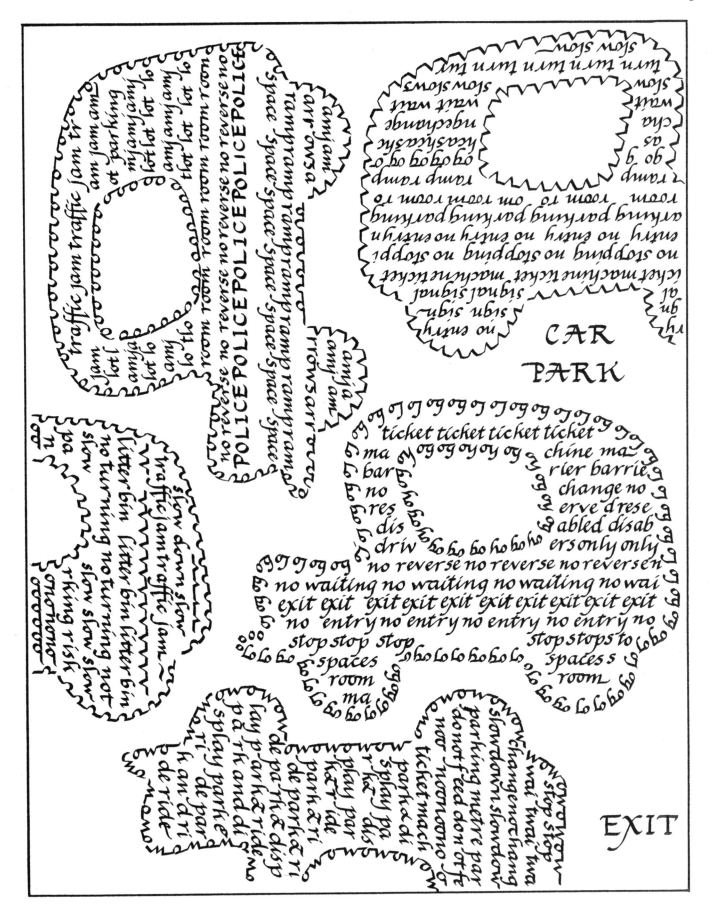

onion

Method: Three 'layers' surround the text. These can be made by making three templates of diminishing size.

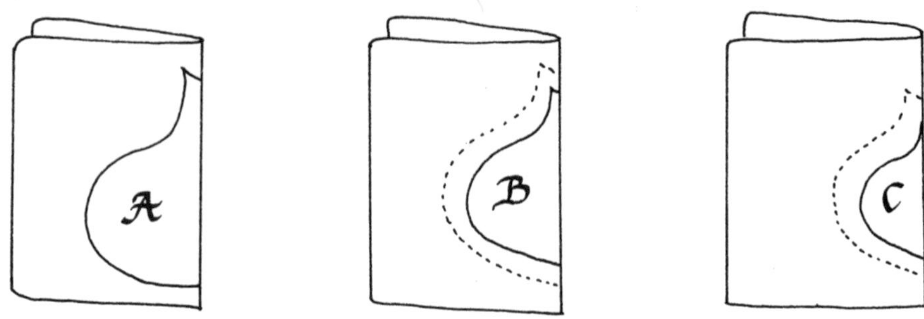

1. Fold a thin card & mark out the outline A. 2. Take a second piece of card. Fold it in two. Mark outline A on this card. Inside the line draw profile B, & cut out the shape. 3. Mark profile B on the third card. Inside this line draw outline C. Cut out the shape. 4. Mark the profile A on your paper. 5. Place shape B inside shape A leaving an even space around it. 6. Inside B place shape C & leave an even space around it. Mark out shape C. 7. Begin at 'x' and make the outline pattern ~ θ: on = three p.w.h. 8. Start at 'y' and make the middle layer θ: o = three p.w.h. 9. From 'z' make the inner layer θ: o = three p.w.h. 10. Draw the outline of the leaves. 11. Complete the outline Δ vv = three p.w.h. 12. Write the text inside the onion: a = three p.w.h. & A = five p.w.h. Δ.

IDEAS: Vegetables can suggest some useful shapes for the calligrapher. The parsnip, turnip & the cabbage all possess bold outlines that could be interpreted with the pen.

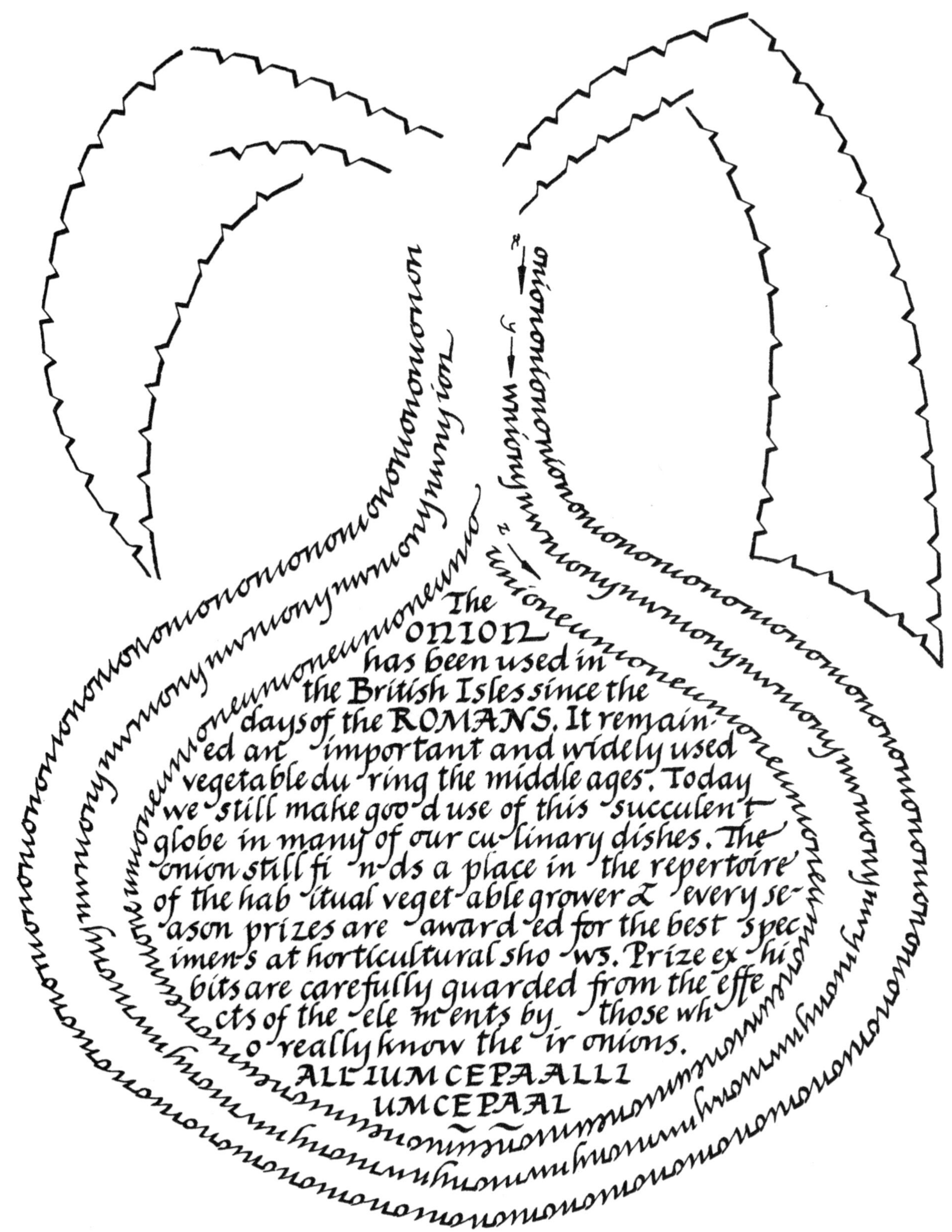
The
ONION
has been used in
the British Isles since the
days of the ROMANS. It remain-
ed an important and widely used
vegetable du-ring the middle ages. Today
we still make goo-d use of this succulent
globe in many of our cu-linary dishes. The
onion still fi-nds a place in the repertoire
of the hab-itual veget-able grower & every se-
ason prizes are award-ed for the best spec-
imen-s at horticultural sho-ws. Prize ex-hi-
bits are carefully guarded from the effects of the ele-m-ents by those wh-
o really know the-ir onions.
ALLIUM CEPA ALLI
UM CEPA AL

θ	PARKER 1/32 ⋀⋀⋀	Δ	OSMIROID MEDIUM V

MESSAGE IN A BOTTLE

Method: 1. Draw the outline. 2. Make the pattern around the outline: vv = two p.w.h. This pattern should be made from the inside of the curve. Begin at 'x'. 3. When the outline vvv is complete finish the bottle top with the ~·~ & SSS strokes. Pen θ. 4. Draw guide lines for the text. These may be made with a flexicurve. Keep the distance between the lines even. 5. With Δ start the text: a = three p.w.h. 6. When the text is complete add the ≈ in the gaps. This device is made with two strokes ~ + ^ = ≈.

Take care to avoid clashing ascenders & descenders. Before you begin practise these running joins.

ƶ liam letter leas

fication continue

IDEAS: Onion-shaped bottles of this kind were made in the C17 - C18. They were made one at a time & so they have individual characteristics. Bottles of this sort can be useful for greeting card designs.

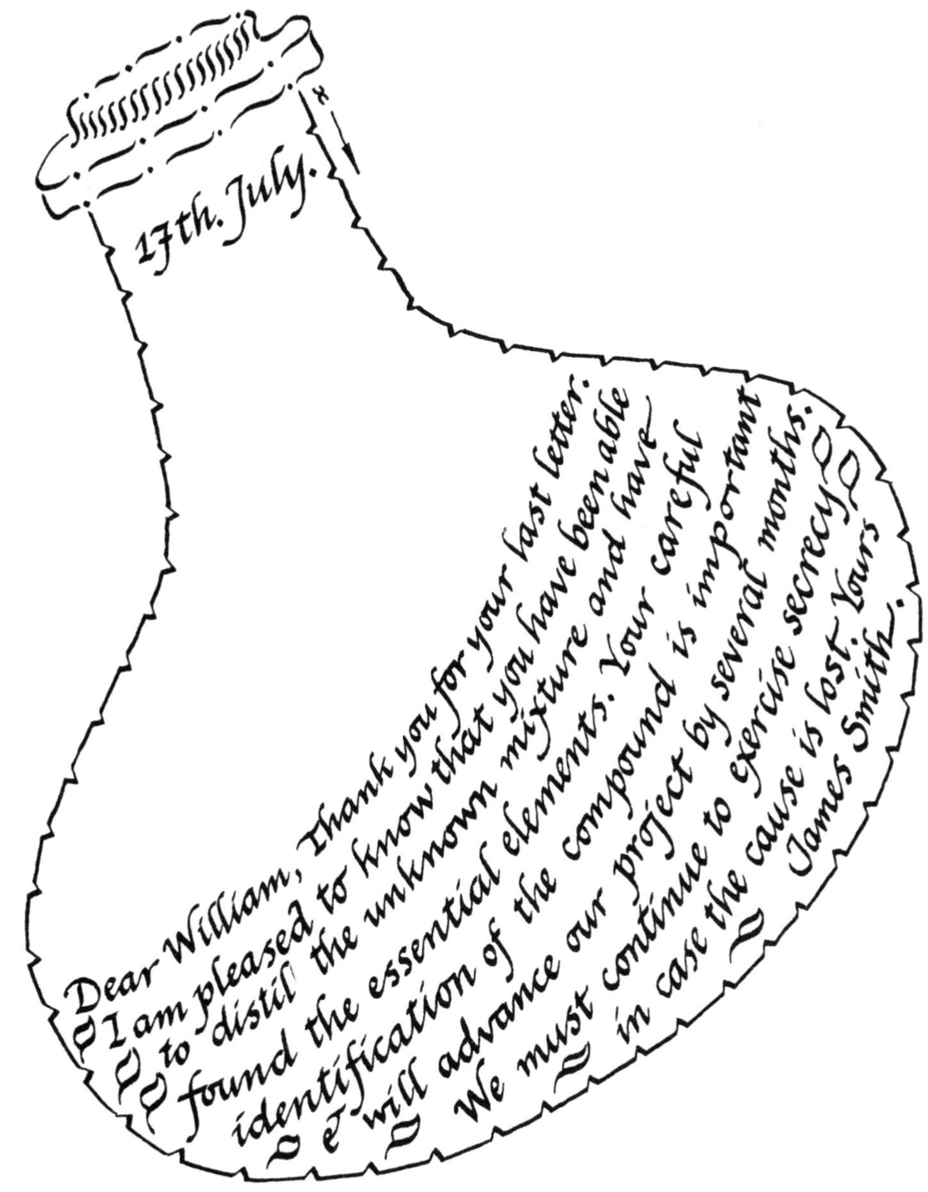
17th. July.
Dear William, Thank you for your last letter.
I am pleased to know that you have been able
to distil the unknown mixture and have
found the essential elements. Your careful
identification of the compound is important
& will advance our project by several months.
We must continue to exercise secrecy
in case the cause is lost. Yours
James Smith.

	PARKER 1/32	Δ	OSMIROID MEDIUM

TOPIARY

Method: 1. Draw the outline shown. 2. Start at 'x' and write the Taxus baccata border: a = three p.w.h. & T = four p.w.h. Pen ϑ. 3. From 'y' make the border around the bird-shape: a = three p.w.h. & B = four p.w.h. Pen ϑ. 4. Using Δ, beginning at the top, write the capitals shown: A = five p.w.h. Notice that these lines rise from left to right. Can you work out why they are arranged in this way? 5. Within the base section complete the intermediate lines: ϑ a = three p.w.h. 6. Reverse the paper and complete the remaining text within the bird. 7. Now add the ground lines using both pens. Make line 'A' first. Then reverse the paper to complete the sequence. 8. Add some ∼ in any large spaces.

In this exercise you will encounter many less familiar words – the Latin names of good topiary species. Practise some of these names on a separate sheet before you begin. Notice the running joins which occur.

ateg monog idata

communis accata

YEW·BOX·PRIVET Make some of the capitals diminish in size.

IDEAS: Find other topiary designs to use. Books about stately homes & gardens can provide helpful illustrations.

Buxus sempervirens Buxus sempervirens Buxus sempervirens

so shaped. Buxus often seen & yew are used. The species ∂ use of it. topiary & made much Various were box

from Rome who first brought the idea to our land. Elizabethan and Jacobean gardeners were very fond of ∂

TOPIARY TOPIARY TOPIARY TOPIARY TOPI

TOPIARIUS. Some writers say that it was the men to describe this pastime comes from the Latin

Pliny the Younger. Our word ∂

TOPIARY TOPIA

as old as ...... tural shapes is at least bs and trees into un-na The art of clipping shru

Taxus baccata Taxus baccata Taxus baccata Taxus baccata Tax

JUNIPERUS COMMUNIS JUNIPER

Crataegus monogyna Crataegus monogyna

LIGUSTRUM LUCIDUM LIGU

Taxus cuspidata Taxus cuspidata Ta

TAXUS BACCATA HIBERN

Rosaceae Rosacea Rosacea Rosace

YEW · BOX · PRIVET · YEW ·

Cupressus sempervirens. Cupre

Cupressus sempervirens Cupre

erus Juniperus communis Ju

WHITETHORN WHIT

Taxus baccata Hibernica Ta

Taxus baccata Hibernica Ta

monogyna monog

Taxus baccata Taxus baccata Taxus baccata

A →

A bird in a nest from Newburgh Priory in North Yorks. near Coxwold.

abcdefghijklmnorstuvwxz abcdefghijklmnorstuvwxz abcde

∂	PARKER 1/32	∨∨∨	Δ	OSMIROID MEDIUM	∨

SWAN

Method: 1. Draw the outline of the swan. 2. Using ⊕ make the outline pattern. Start at 'x'. 3. With π and starting at 'a' begin the body text: a = three p.w.h. Do not allow any ascending/descending strokes to clash. Reverse the paper to make the alphabet down the neck. 4. With Δ make the two rows of ccc's below the figure: c = five p.w.h. 5. Use π to make the 'swan of Thames' line: a = four p.w.h. 6. The next two lines are made with Δ: c = five p.w.h. & A = five p.w.h. 7. The last line is made with π – see 3 above. 8. With Δ make the headline pattern: vv = two p.w.h. 9. Add the names A = four p.w.h. 10. Make the lower row of pattern – repeat 8. 11. Make the lower border by repeating 8, 9 & 10.

A number of Welsh words are used in the text.

cyw alarch — cygnet

alarch — swan

Make these strokes first. ſſ Then add → ffrwd — stream

nofio — swim

llithro — glide

pluen — feather

padlo — paddle

rhodli — paddle

---

swanheards
Dyers Vintners
mute Bewick Royal
R. Thames swanr swan
upper swan upping sw
ana zwaan cygnus olo
r cygnus mansuetus cy
gnus schwanc swanaz
cygnus zwaan svan
swana svanr zwaa
cygnusc cygnus cygnus cyg
svanr swanaz swana zwaan sv anr swa
schwanc cygnus melanocoryphus cygnus mu
sicus cygnus colambianus cygnus colombi
anus cygnus ferus cygnus nigricollis
cygnus americanus cygnus svan
cygnus gibbus cygnus mansuet

To think one's geese all swans. Rom. & Juliet. I. II. 92.
The swan of Avon.

IDEAS: Reverse the shape & find another text. Look in atlas & discover more swan names.

Try this alternative swan.

Use some colours.

SWANBOURNE · SWANLAND · SWANLEY · SWANMORE ·

cy
cyw
a lar
cywala
cywalarc
cywalarchen
schwanpadl nofio pluen pad
hodi lli throty ala rch sc hw
pluenpluenpluenpluenpluen
ffrwd ffrwd ffrwd ffrwd ffrw
nofi nofi nofi nofi nofio swan
plue plue plue pluen plue pluen p
nofi padlo rhodi padl hodi plue hodi
p luen alarchalr chalarcha larchalarch alarc
cygnus cygnets schwan cygnet cygnus cygnets schwan sc
padlc ywalarch plu en pl uen pl uen plue
rhodi nofi onofio no fio nofi o nofi o nofio n
llithr oswi swim swim swims swim sw
archen stream stream streamstr
cccccccccccccccccccccccccc
cccccccccccccccccccccccccccccc
swan of Thames swan of Avon swan of Thames swan
ccccc cccccccccc cccccccc ccccccccccc
SWANUPPING SWANUPPING SWANUPPING SWANUP
swimcygnet swim paddle with the stream swim cygnet swim swimsw

SWANNINGTON · SWANSCOMBE · SWANSEA · SWANTON

θ	PARKER 1/32	π	OSMIROID MED.	Δ	OSMIROID BROAD

STADDLE STONE

Method: 1. Draw the lines A–F in pencil. 2. Starting with A make the outline pattern ⊕ vv = two p.w.h. 3. Complete the remaining lines in order B–F. To write D, E & F turn the paper upside down. 4. Make the four rows of unjoined letters starting at G: a = three p.w.h. 5. Start the CAPITALS △: A = four p.w.h. 6. Begin the text ⌘ which is condensed: ⊕ (A = five p.w.h.) & (a = three p.w.h.). Take care with the letter shapes & work slowly. 7. Write the title ⊕ : (A = five p.w.h.).

Ideas: Try using grey ink for this design. You can make a light grey darker by adding some black. A two-tone grey effect can be achieved in this way.

Try the flat version of the staddle stone shown below.

Use an alternative outline in a contrasting colour.

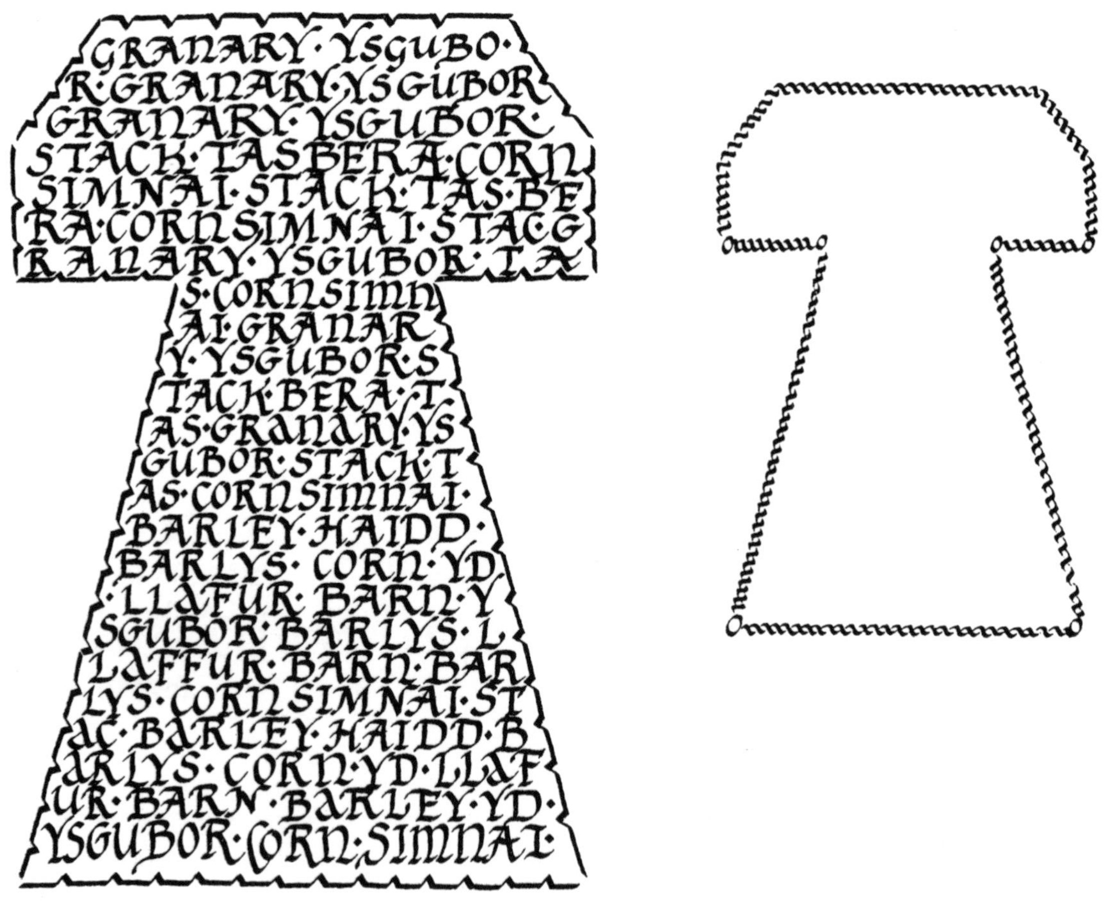

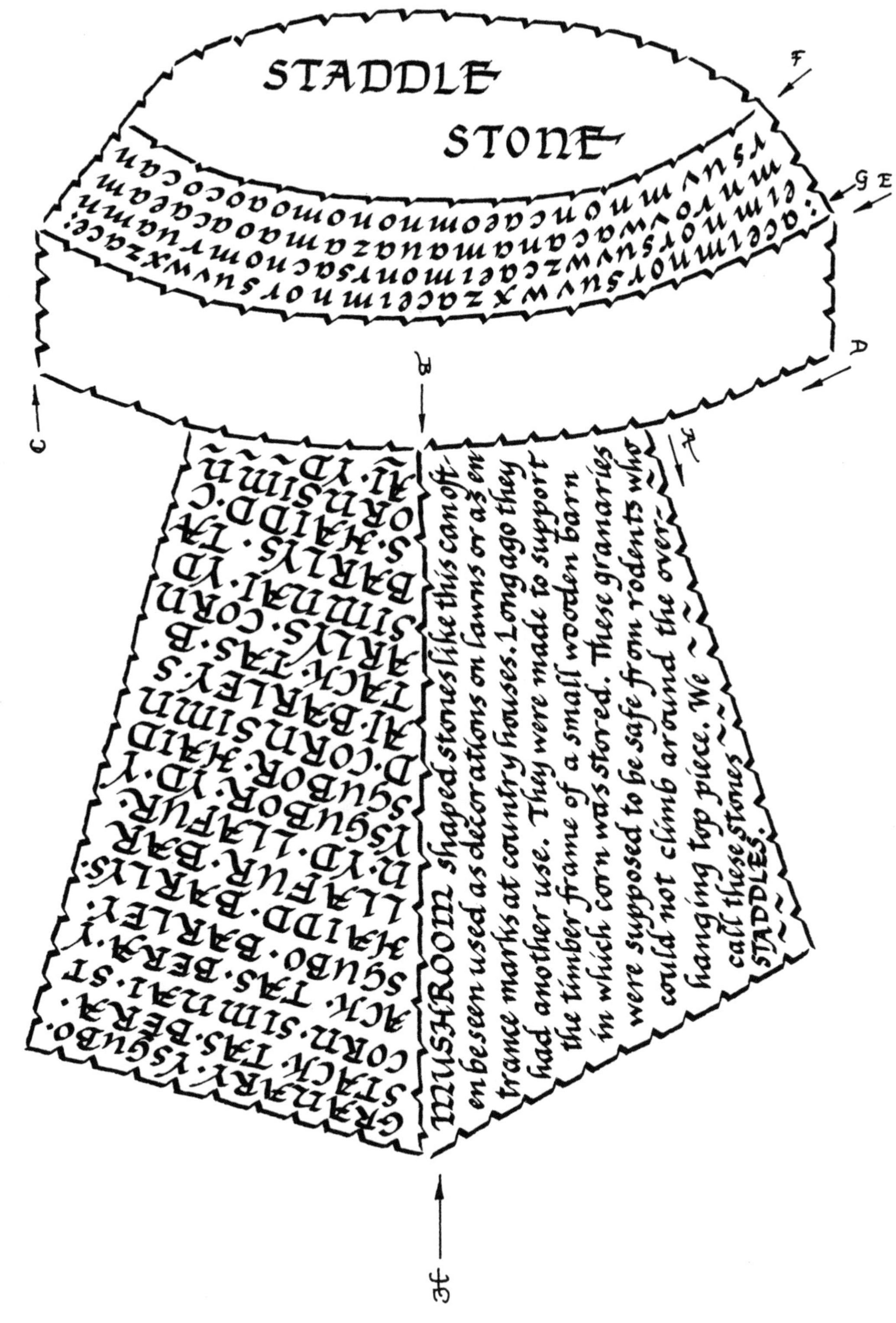

	PARKER 1/32	Δ	OSMIROLD MED.

LONGSHIP

Method: 1. Draw the outline of the ship. 2. With ϑ begin at 'x' & make the vv's two p.w.h. 3. Make the line 'y' at the other end. 4. From 'z' link the previous lines with vv's = two p.w.h. 5. Use Δ to make the capitals which form the mast. 6. Start at ϕ and make the two rows of capitals: ϑ A = three p.w.h. 7. Add the sails, VV = two p.w.h., & then make the dots. 8. In the sternpost make the lower case letters shown. Begin at 'x' with Δ : a = three p.w.h. 9. At the opposite end make the text shown: ϑ a = three p.w.h. 10. Make the text inside the ship's hull ~ start at "AEGIR" : a = three p.w.h. & A = five p.w.h. 11. With Δ add the dots between the text. 12. At the bow of the ship make the five lines of ccc's with Δ c = three p.w.h. 13. Between these letters form the smaller ccc's shown = three p.w.h. 14. Use a flexicurve to draw the five lines at the base. 15. With ϑ copy the text shown: a = three p.w.h. & A = five p.w.h. 16. Complete the design by adding ~ or ✑ as desired.

Try some of these capitals before you begin. F A

V S S S S

D E The s can take various forms. N O

IDEAS: Viking art has many shapes to offer a calligrapher. The Viking exhibition at York ~ 'JORVIK' ~ is worth a visit. Richard Hall's 'The Viking Dig' (1984) is a useful reference.

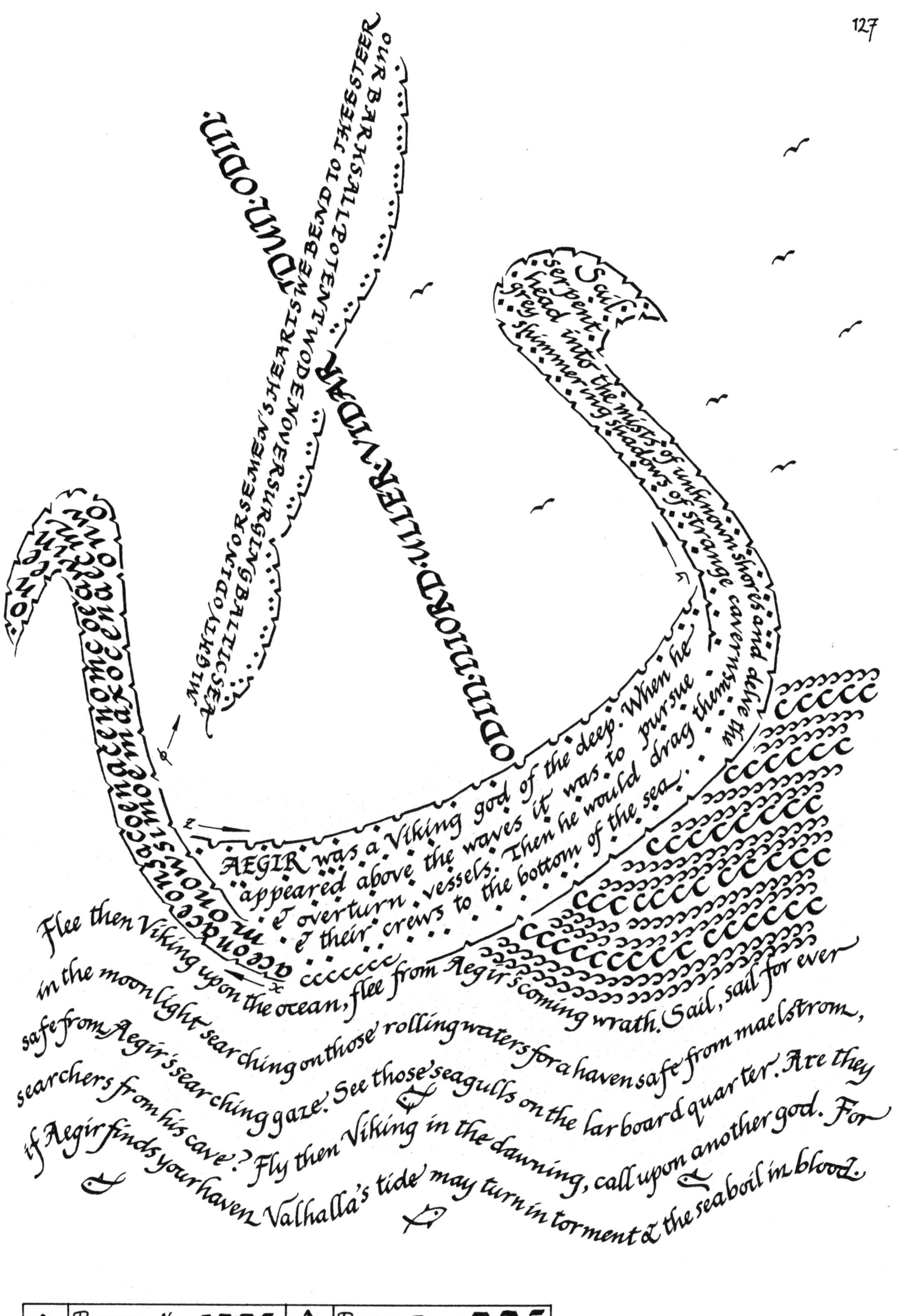

⊘	PARKER 1/32	Δ	PARKER BROAD

ELEPHANT

Method: 1. Draw the outline of the shape. 2. Draw the tusks. in ink. 3. Start at A and make the outline pattern vv = three p.w.h. θ. 4. From B draw the outline of the trunk. 5. Begin at C & write the outline of the ear. Complete the position of the eye. 6. At D begin the text which is not in exactly straight lines but "fits" together. 7. Complete the ground lines.

IDEAS: Use colours to emphasise the outline.

With wider pens replace the text with a range of textures in the manner shown below. Try a range of colours.

	PARKER 1/32

BOOKPLATES

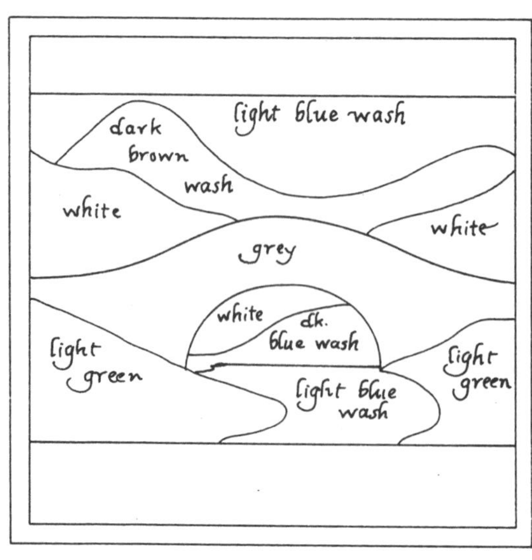

Before you begin a design make a rough diagram so that you can see where the dark & light areas will meet.
Look at the textures in the above example & translate them into the colours suggested in the diagram.

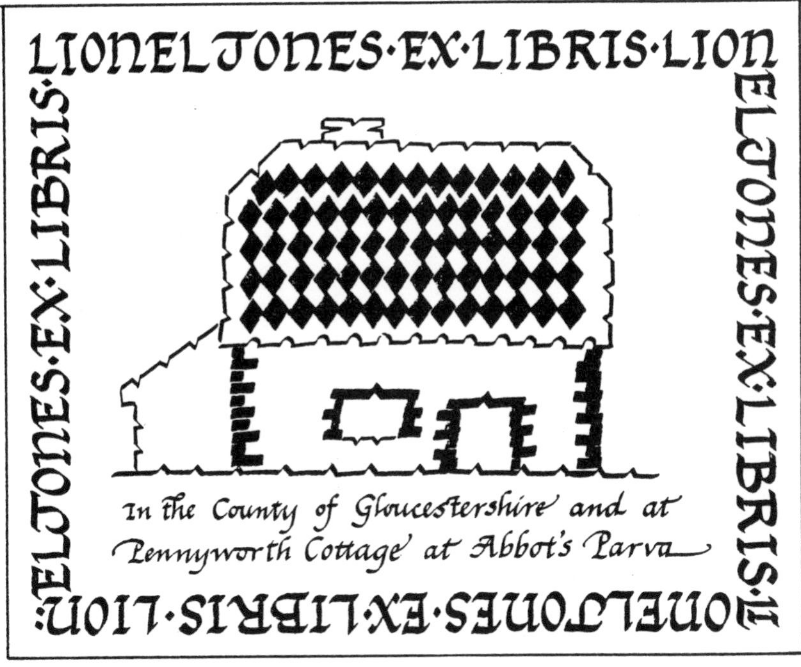

BOOKPLATES can be useful subjects for the calligrapher. The subject does allow 'patterns' to be used. In this example broad nibs have been employed for the border text - with few gaps - & the textures applied to the cottage. Notice the way in which small gaps are left between some pen strokes - left hand side - to make 'white' lines. The lozenge ◆ shapes on the roof can best be made by working across in lines. It is more difficult to make a regular pattern if you work vertically. The door/window shapes could be made solid black. The proportions of these examples were determined by the shape of the cottage. Invent some other designs which are taller than they are wide.

Sometimes a simple design can be equally effective. without a border that has a 'heavy' content. Two broad nibs were used for the titles. They help to alter the 'weight' of a design.

BOOKMARKS

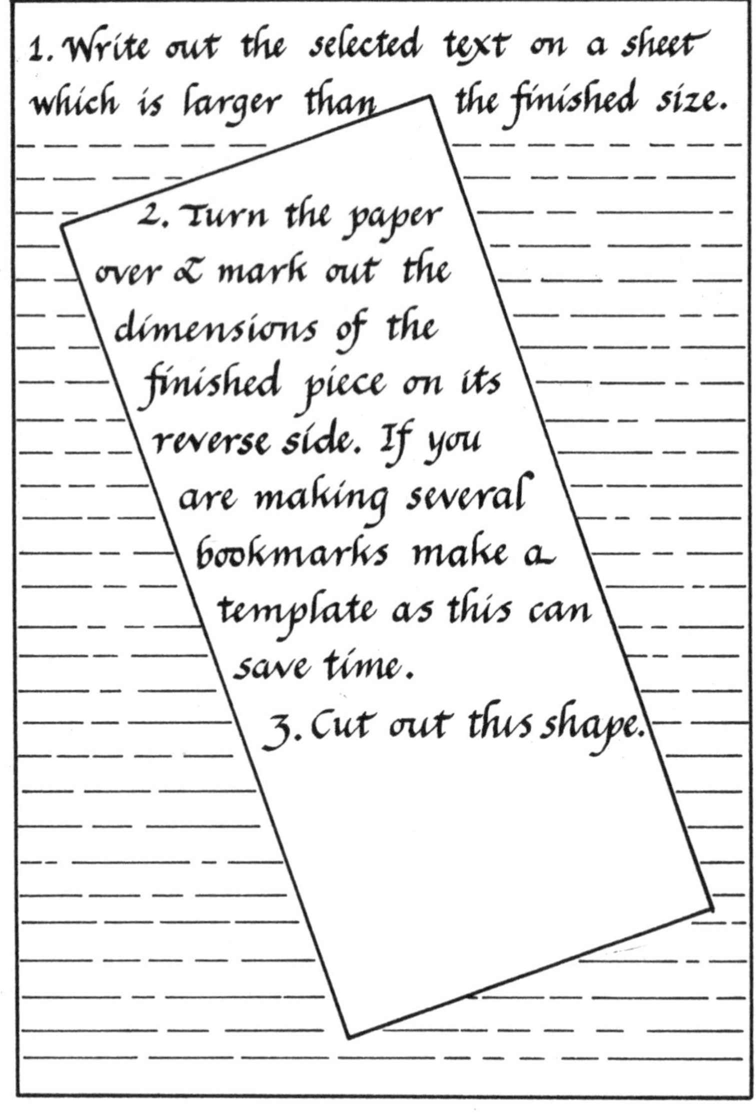

1. Write out the selected text on a sheet which is larger than the finished size.
2. Turn the paper over & mark out the dimensions of the finished piece on its reverse side. If you are making several bookmarks make a template as this can save time.
3. Cut out this shape.

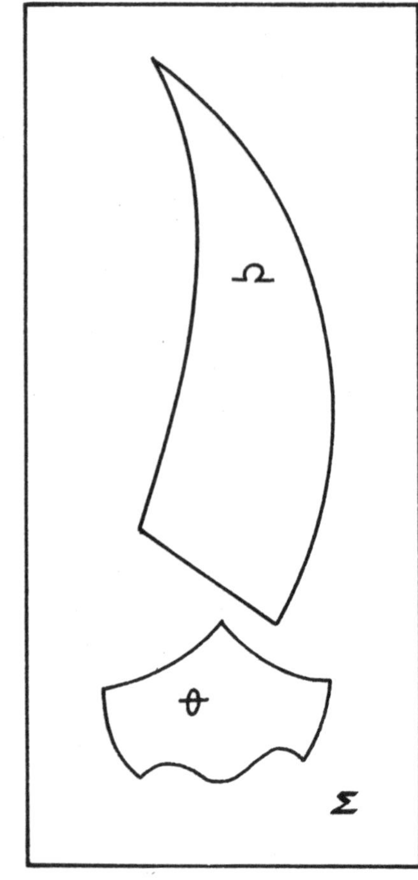

4. With the written surface face down sketch in the above shapes with a soft pencil.

5. Use a fine knife & cut out the shapes θ & Ω from the finished bookmark. 6. To make 'A' stick the shape Σ to a thicker & larger card of contrasting colour. Spray adhesive is a useful medium. 7. To make 'B' cut a suitable sized card. 8. Add adhesive to θ and place it on 'B'. 9. Repeat the process for Ω. 10. To protect the finished work fix a clear self adhesive film to both sides of 'A' & 'B'.

REVERSING THE IMAGE

To make these bookmarks follow the instructions opposite.

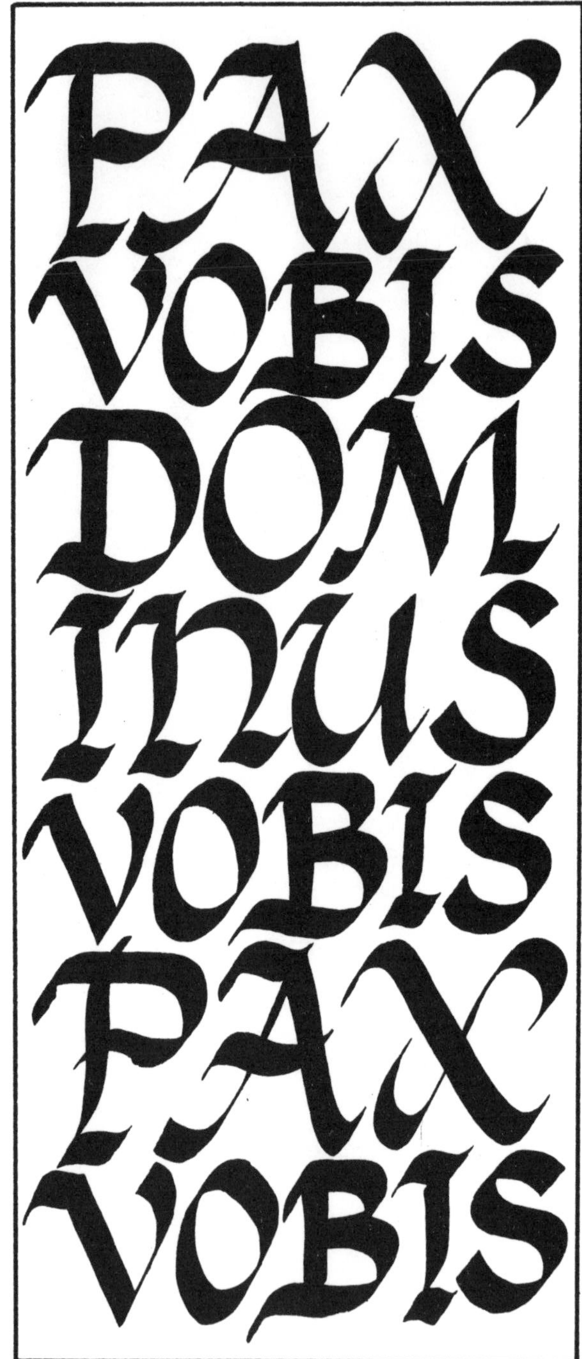
PAX
VOBIS
DOM
INUS
VOBIS
PAX
VOBIS

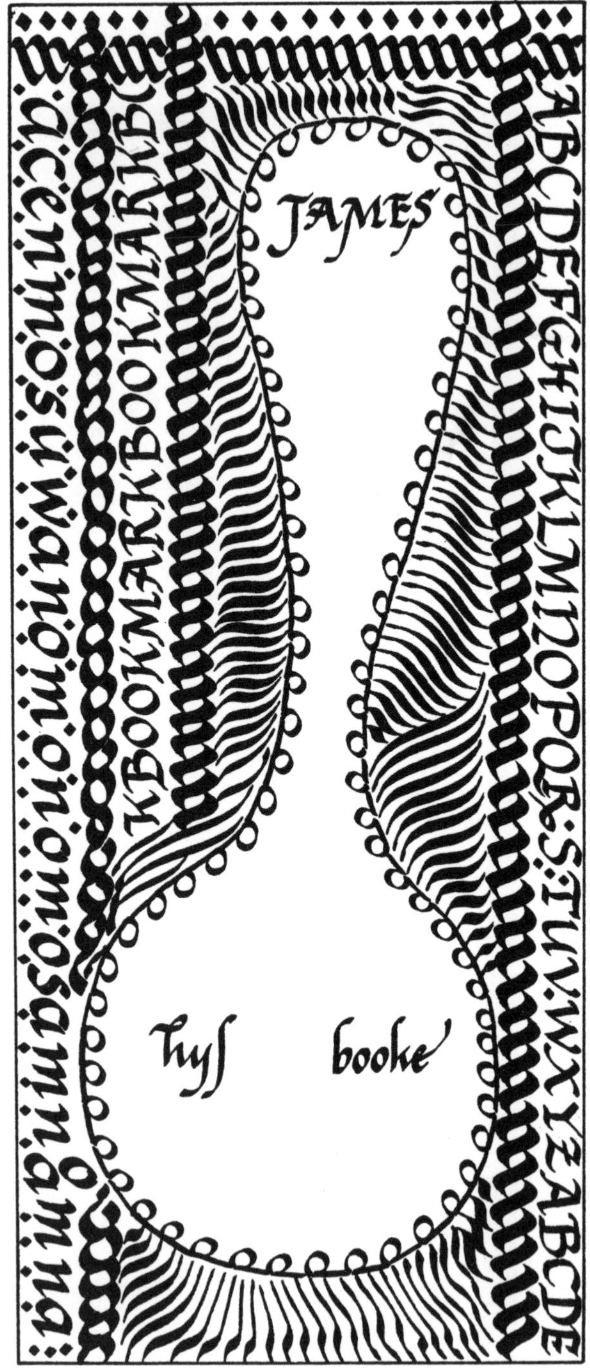
JAMES
thys booke

ABCDEE
FGHIJK
FGHIJK
ABCDE
LMNOP
LIBRUM
QRSTU
HUNC·
VWXYZ
CARPE
CARPE·
VWXYZ
HUNC·LI
QRSTU
BRUM·CA
KLMNO·
RPE·HUN
EFGHIJ
C·LIBRU
M·ABCD

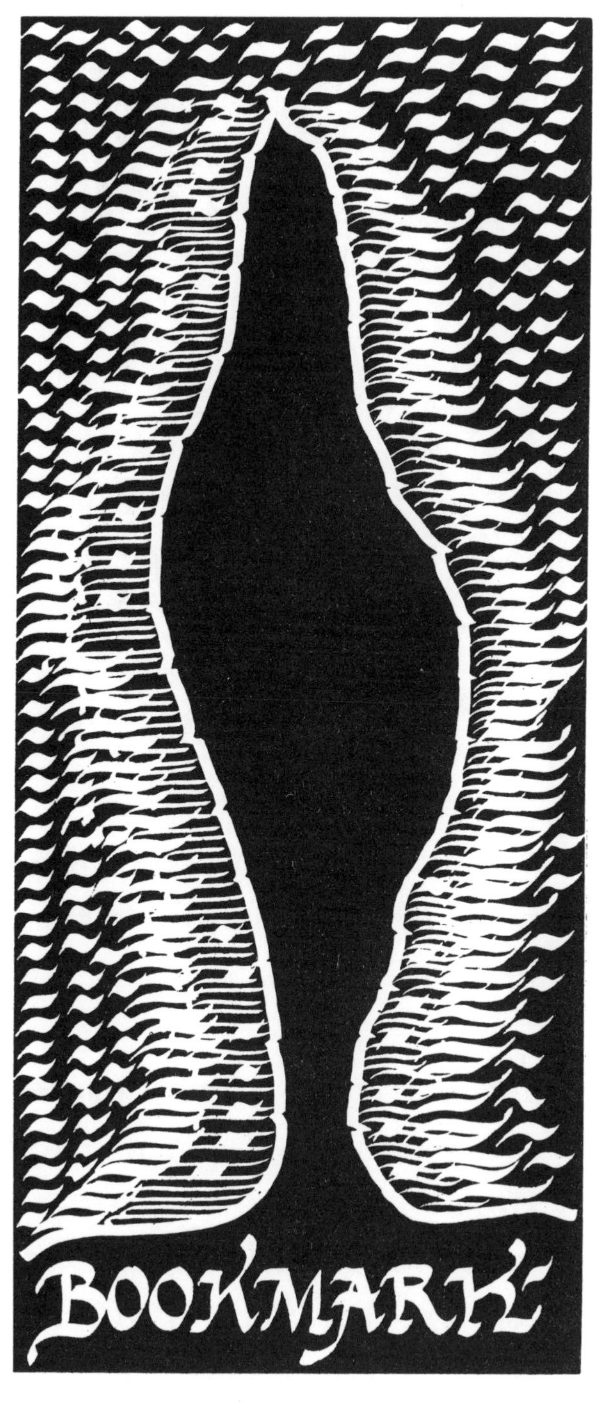

White ink on a dark or coloured ground can also be effective. Shake or stir the ink thoroughly before you begin.

GREETINGS CARDS

The making of greeting cards can be rewarding. Methods of reproduction will allow a single design to be replicated cheaply. Single colour reproduction is much cheaper & you can always add a colourwash to the black printed version. If you choose a coloured card this will give you two-colour design & you can add a third tint yourself. This example uses an amalgamation of simple ideas. Notice the two spellings of HALLELUJAH, the angel figure – made with a shadow nib, & the heavier renderings of Alpha & Omega Ω. To the black/white version you could add colour to the area surrounding the angel & between the lines ᐯᐯ & ᐱᐱ.

The fir tree has become a symbol of Christmas. This design also uses the Welsh version of 'Merry Christmas'. The text could be rendered in contrasting colours – red/black, or alternate lines could be counterchanged.

From an idea by Lindsay Penny.

REDUCED FROM $5\frac{1}{2}$" DIA.

This design is based upon a simple geometrical pattern which divides the circle into 16 ~ $22\frac{1}{2}^\circ$ ~ segments ; one for each large letter. There are five concentric circles to provide guidelines for the different elements. In place of the alphabetical sequence you could use the text 'UNTO US A BOY IS BORN'. Draw the diagram to the required size & use it as an underlay to rough out your version on detail paper. Start with the inner letters & then form the larger ones. Then add the petals & finish with the dots at the centre. Notice that these have a variable density. Try black & two other colours for your own design.

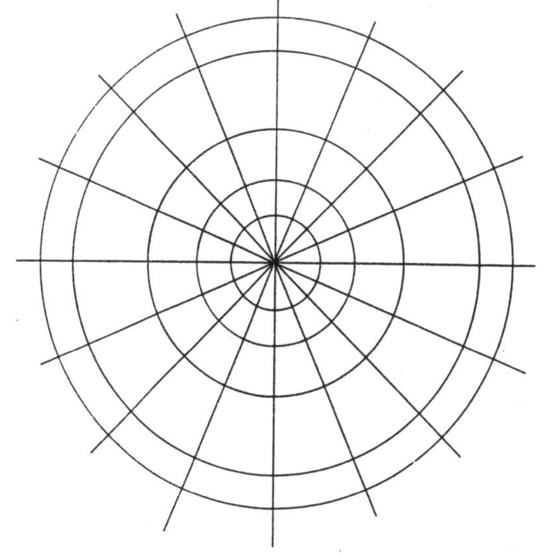

LANDSCAPES

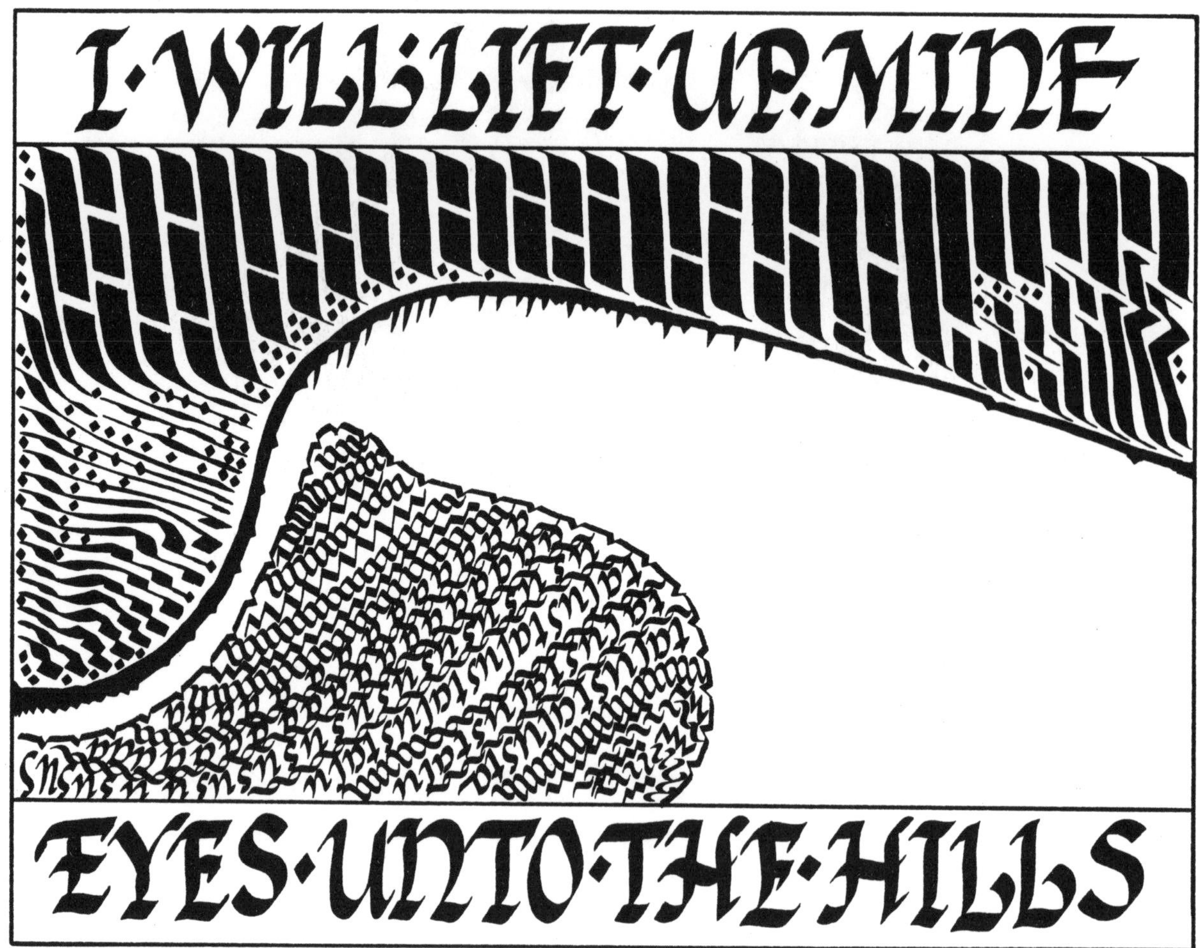
I·WILL·LIFT·UP·MINE
EYES·UNTO·THE·HILLS

Landscapes can provide ideas for the calligrapher. Do not make designs too complicated. This example has three main areas with defined divisions. When colours are used even simple examples of this kind can be effective. Textures can be varied by using several pens of different widths. Use the wider nibs first & work downwards to finer pens.

The text, from Psalm 121, was made with two pens – the wider nib was used for the lower line. Psalms & Proverbs can supply many suitable texts for designs of this kind.

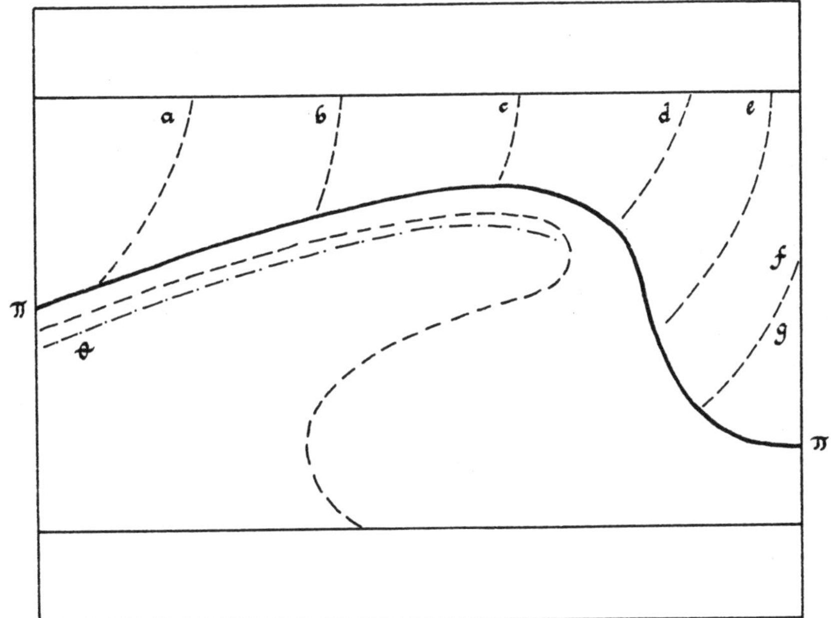

Reversing the image changes the effect. Make the area above line π~π several different colours ~ grey, blue, red, yellow etc. The hillside θ could be arranged in sepia furrows. Try making a, c, e, g the same colour.

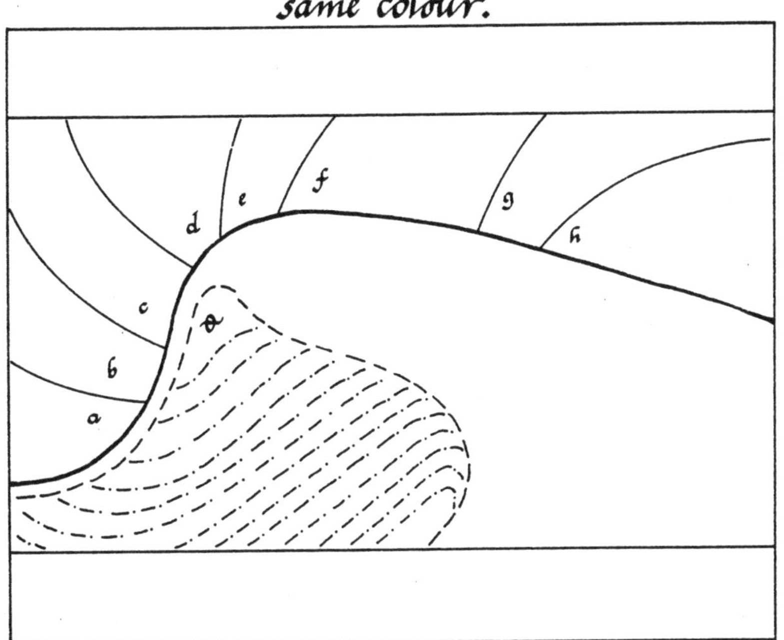

Compare this outline with the example opposite. Make the sky patterns change direction within the areas a~h & grade the colours from light to dark. Try grey & sepia alternately in the area θ. Find another text for the top & bottom.

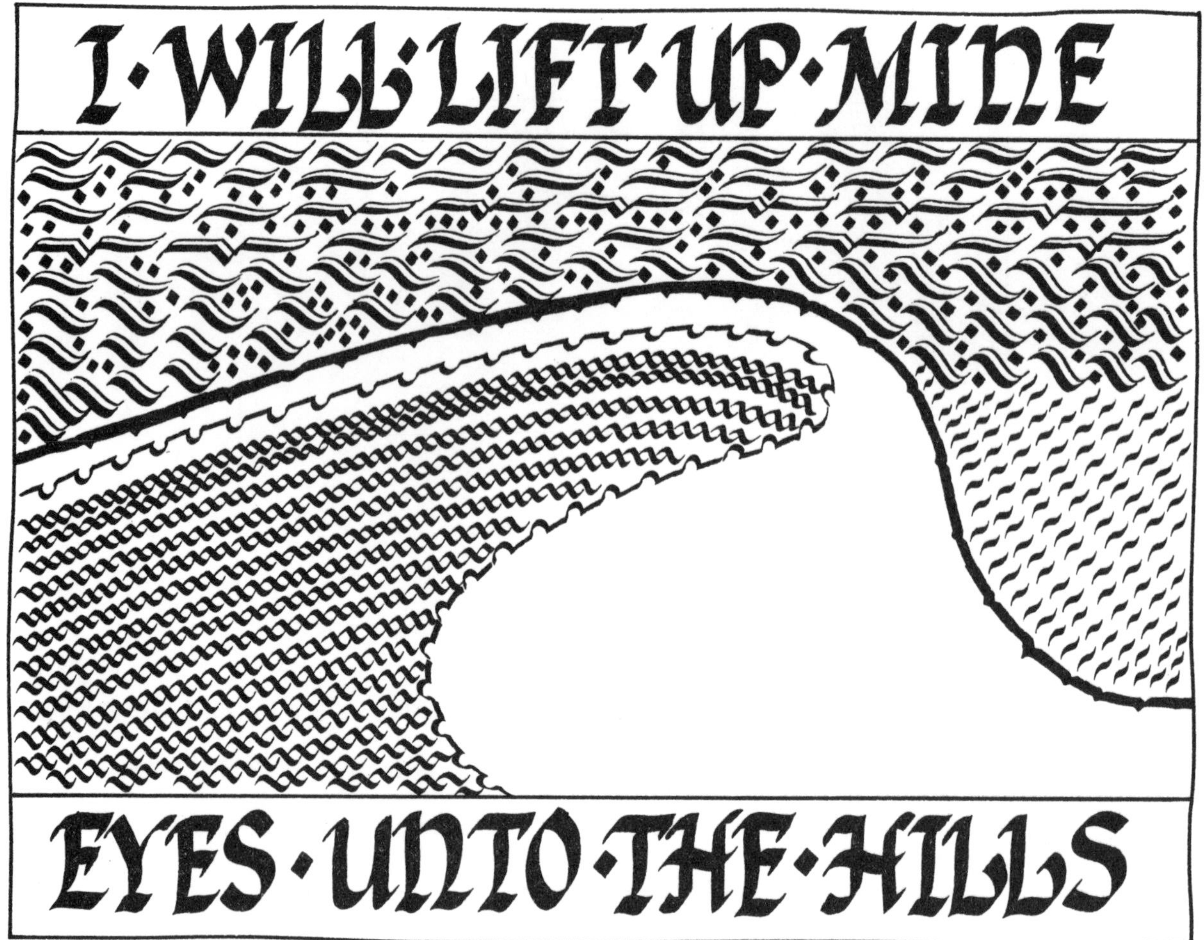

I·WILL·LIFT·UP·MINE
EYES·UNTO·THE·HILLS

Turning the shape upside down alters its appearance. The lines show the direction of the patterns. Use three colours for b, d & f. Below line A-A the patterns are placed in herringbone fash-ion g to l. Notice the differences in line spacing. For g-l use dark colours to contrast with b, d & f.

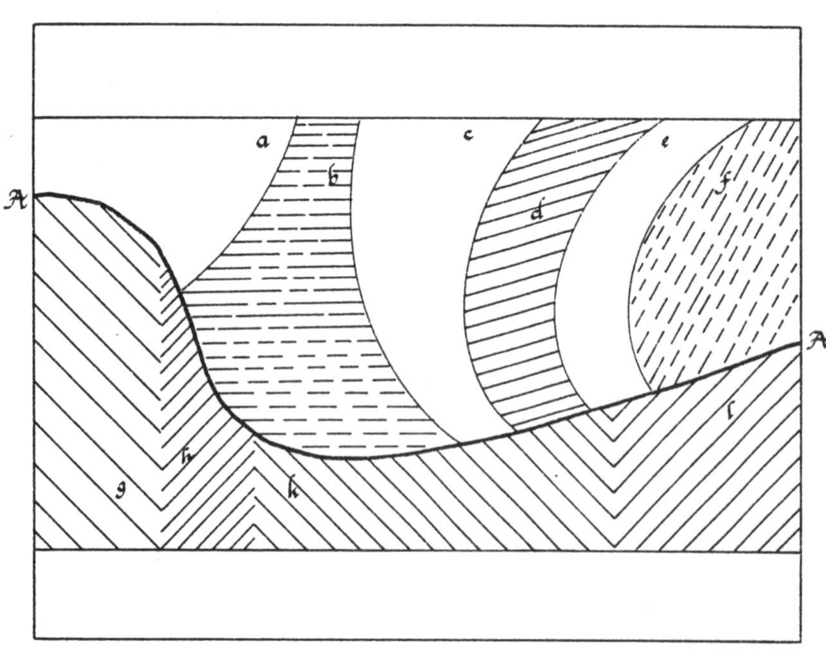

Empty shapes can also make effective designs. This example is based on the outline of a famous Cornish landmark called the Cheesewring,

near St. Cleer. The Book of Proverbs, a rich source of quotes, provides the text & the main idea. When you have drawn the outline use a blue pencil to sketch in the main divisions of the textured area. This subject is suitable for colourwork ~ see diagrams below. The alternative version moves the subject to the right. Try a design with the subject reversed. You will need several pens.

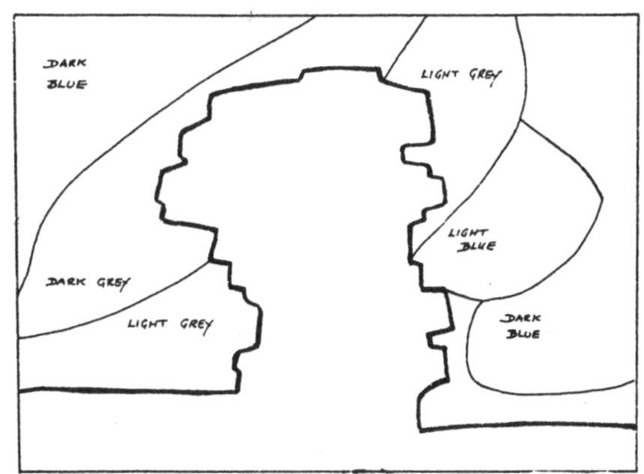

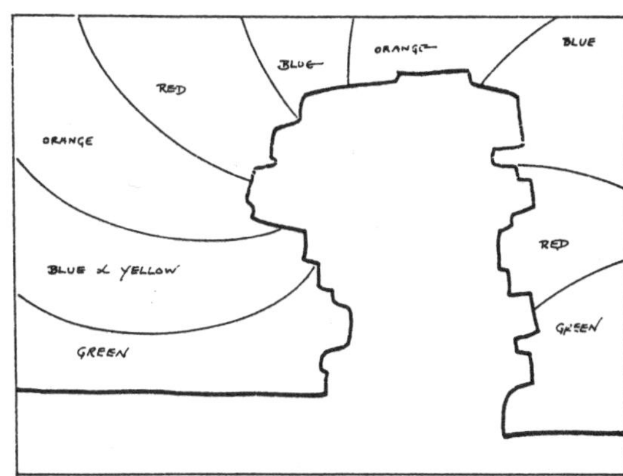

MAPS

Cartographers have found many ways of decorating their work. Local historians frequently uncover fascinating details about particular places & the fruits of their studies can often be illustrated in a graphic form. The example shown opposite was devised by using several pens – including a barrel pen. Maps of this kind can usefully contain illustrations. If you are not confident about drawing then you can enlist the help of an artist to do this part of the work. Old estate or village maps will often record the names of land-property owners or occupiers. To avoid crowding the map information of this kind can be shown as a table – which needs to be given a key – like the one shown here with numbers 1–15. Mapmakers are fond of landmarks & these can add interest to any design. Maps can record today's world too. Try a version of your own locality. A single street will supply good material for the pen's interpretation. Do not forget the lanes – entrances which lead off a thoroughfare. An excellent example of work of this kind is 'A Walk around the Snickleways of York' by Mark Jones – available from the author at: April Cottage, Bulmer, York, YO6 7BW.

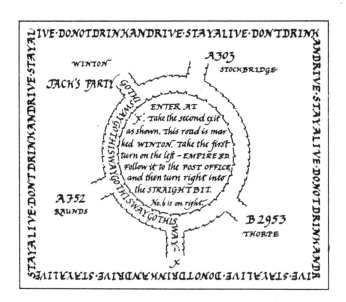

Maps can also be used to give directions to visitors not familiar with a given place. This example shows the way to a party.

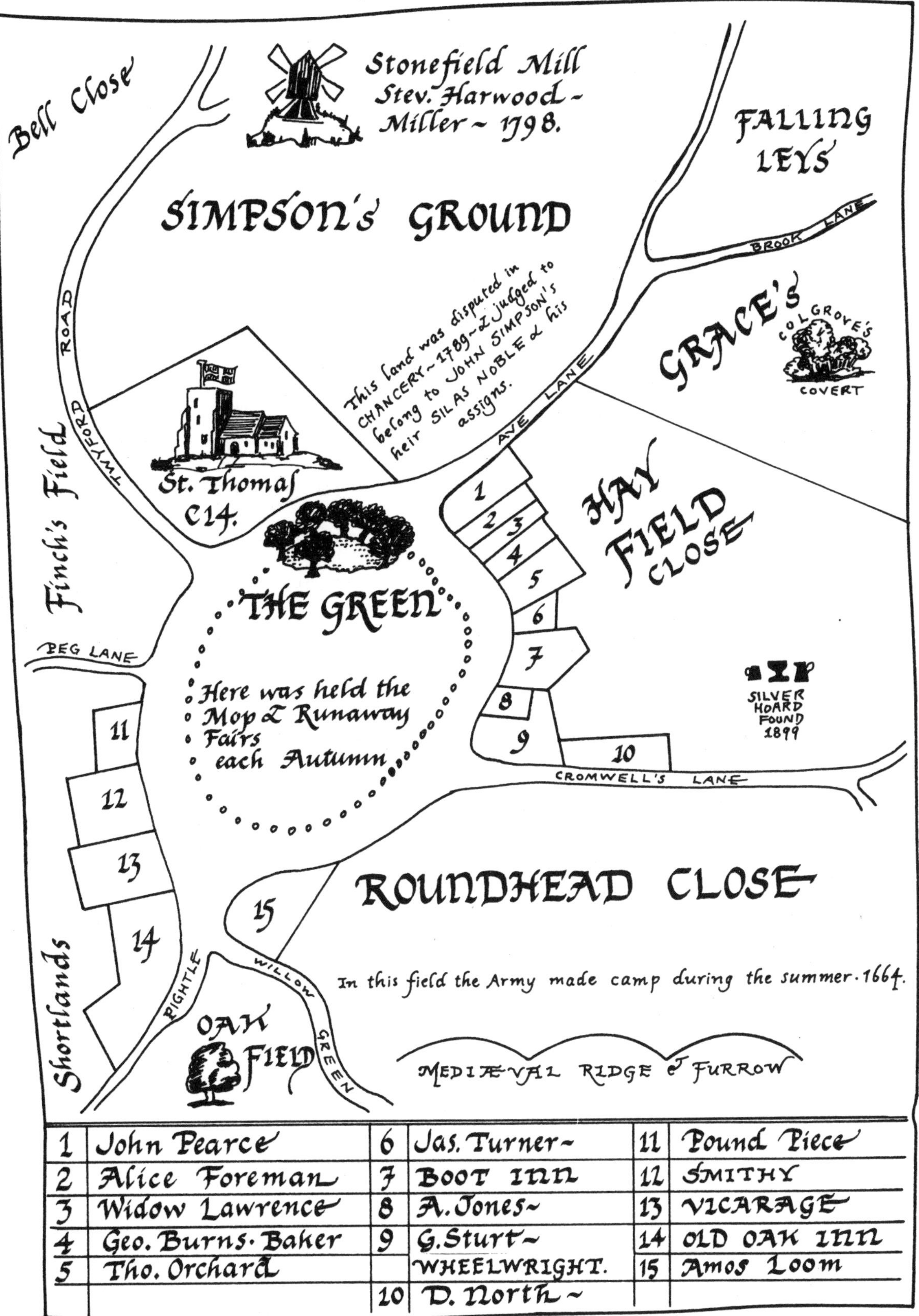

1	John Pearce	6	Jas. Turner~	11	Pound Piece
2	Alice Foreman	7	BOOT INN	12	SMITHY
3	Widow Lawrence	8	A. Jones~	13	VICARAGE
4	Geo. Burns. Baker	9	G. Sturt~	14	OLD OAK INN
5	Tho. Orchard		WHEELWRIGHT.	15	Amos Loom
		10	D. North~		

GRACE

This example shows the effect of reducing a design by fifty six per cent. This makes it the size of an A6 standard size card.

For These
& all hys mercies
WE PRAISE GOD'S
HOLY NAME
THROUGH
JESUS CHRIST
OUR LORD
AMEN AMEN
B.W.S.
A GRACE · CULHAM COLLEGE · OXON ·

When you are calculating the amount of reduction you need to measure the diagonal of the original. A reduction of 50% will result in an area one quarter of the original as the diagram shows.

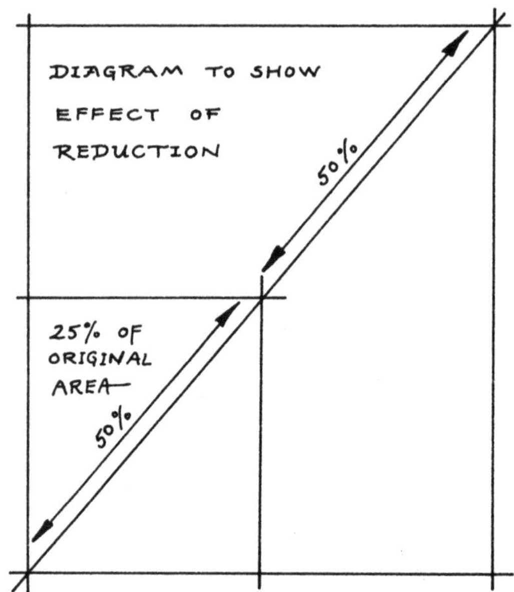

Several pens were used for this version of a College Grace. The plainsong stave provides the framework for the text. Draw this first & then select the pens you wish to use (the original was made with Osmiroid B10, B6 & a 'Shadow' B6 nibs).

Spacing out a text needs patience & you may expect to spend about a day working out the details of such a design.

Try this example in black & red, or red & blue.

For These
& all hys mercies

WE PRAISE GOD's
HOLY NAME

THROUGH
JESUS CHRIST
OUR LORD

B.W.S.

·AMEN·AMEN·

A GRACE · CULHAM COLLEGE · OXON ·

FAMILY TREE

Everyone has ancestors and there is a great interest in family history. This example represents just one way in which a group of relationships can be expressed. The widest nib was used for the basic family name & subsequent branches are rendered in nibs of decreasing size.

Before you begin a design of this kind draw a rough diagram like the one above to give you a guide to placing the main name elements. Different colours can be introduced to help emphasise separate branches. When all the names have been recorded add the decorative leaves & patterns.

Here are some alternative tree shapes to try out. Supply your own names.

SMITH

BENSON

PARRY

WILLIAMS

CROMPTON

JACOBS

JAMES

PERKINS

ARNOLD

ANDREWS

Alexander Marie Alec Column

Sally Edward Bess

Jane Edward Paul

Peter Charles Tom

Sarah Adrian

Tristan

Paul Thomas

Liam Timothy

Susan

Jason Mary

Roshanne

Amanda Clotilda

Patrick Sean

Elizabeth Ann Ray

Janet Clive

Albert Anne

Margaret Ann

Sophie Clive

James Simon

Peter Penelope

Ronald

Brenda Bernard

Josiah Amos

Susan Brian Vikki

BORDERS: Various forms of writing can be enhanced by adding a border. Borders do not have to completely surround a text.

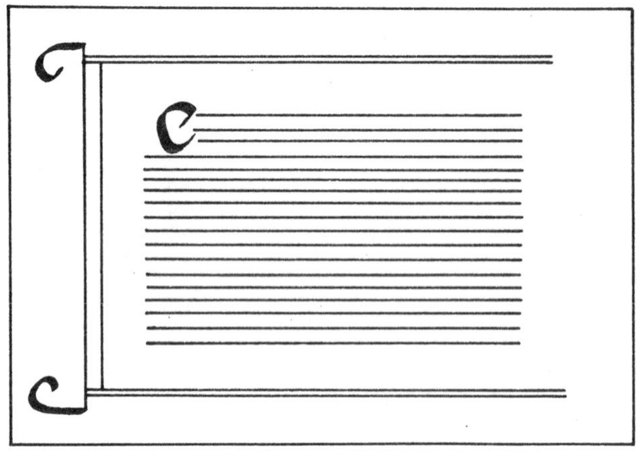

A principal left-hand border with minor lines at top & bottom.

The all-round border with a text arranged centrally.

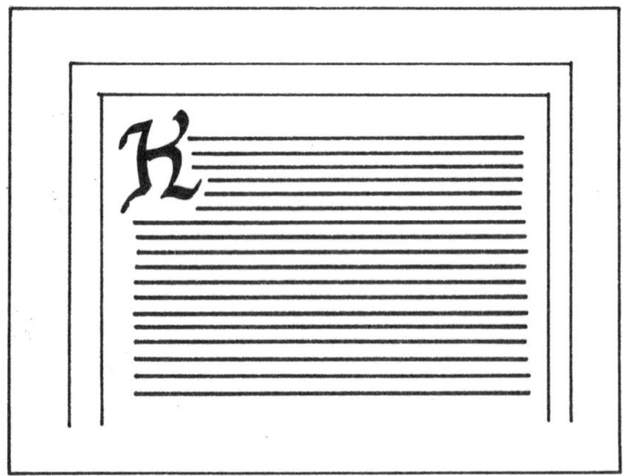

A three-sided border.

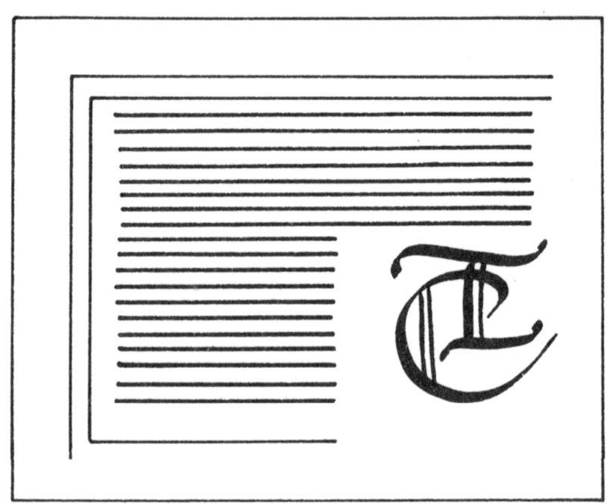

An asymmetrical three-sided border.

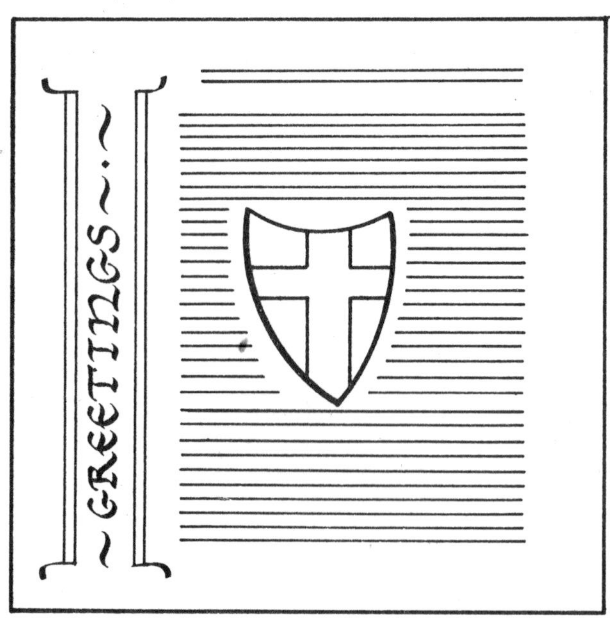

Border of CAPITALS & TEXT surrounding an illustration.

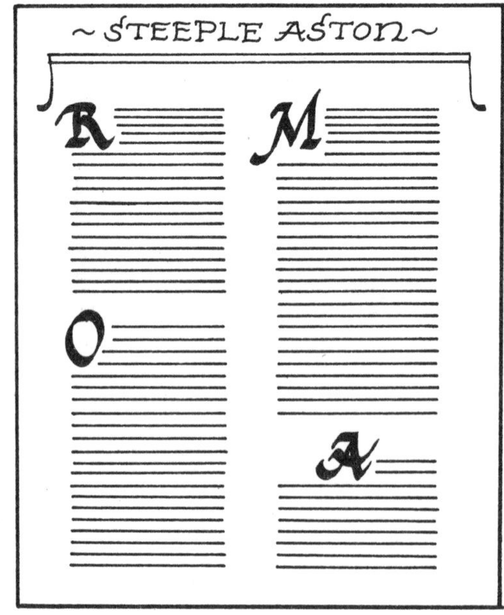

A headline border.

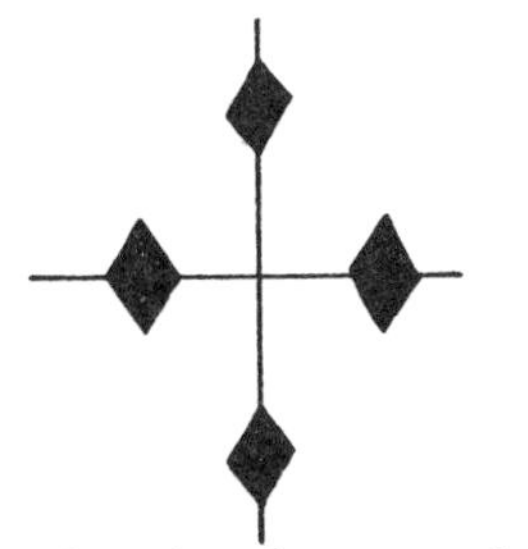

A broad nib can make these lozenge-shaped dots. Use the edge of the nib to make the thin strokes.

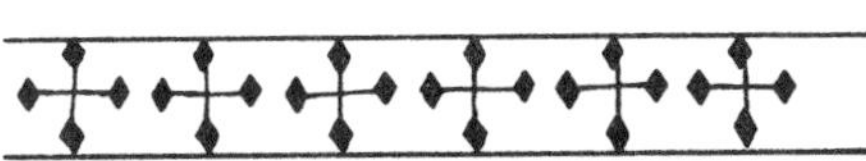

ON a smaller scale a row of CROSSES can make a good border. The verticals & horizontals do not have to be equal.

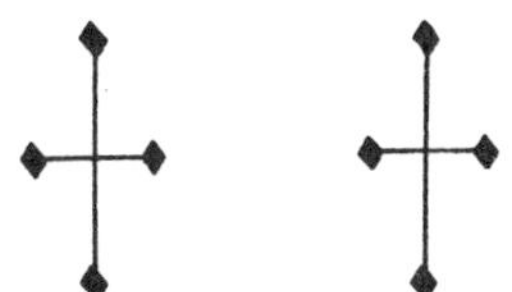

THE simple downstroke can be used to make patterns like this. A dot can separate the main elements & add to the texture.

TO MAKE a + b TURN PAPER UPSIDE DOWN.

Two pens are used for this border. Construct the lines in the order shown. Practise 'b' before you start.

Use two pens: 1 + 2 = a broad nib. Line 3 = fine.

Use two pens: a + d = fine ; b + c = broad. Practise 'b' before you begin. Lines a + d could vary in height.

ANOTHER FLORAL BORDER.

THIS STYLE OF BORDER CAN BE EFFECTIVE IN TWO COLOURS. Line 6 could be made with a finer nib.

THIS BORDER CAN BE MADE WITH TWO PENS. STROKES 2 + 3 are made with the fine edge. THE SPACE 'x' CAN BE DECORATED WITH A TEXT.

THE A + V shapes are useful elements for borders, which do not always need a LINEAR outline.

THE A WITHOUT A CROSS BAR PROVIDES AN ANTIQUE LOOK.

REVERSED ALTERNATE LETTERS COULD BE MADE IN TWO COLOURS.

A SIMPLE IDEA FOR TWO PENS.

BOLD DOTS MADE WITH 5mm FELT PENS CAN FORM INTERESTING BORDERS.

VARIOUS FORMS OF THE AMPERSAND CAN BE USED FOR BORDERS.

TWO FACING LINES.

WITH ADDED INITIALS.

VARIATIONS of E & E.

OPEN E's & REVERSALS.

A LEAF DESIGN WITH CAPITALS: use contrasting colours.

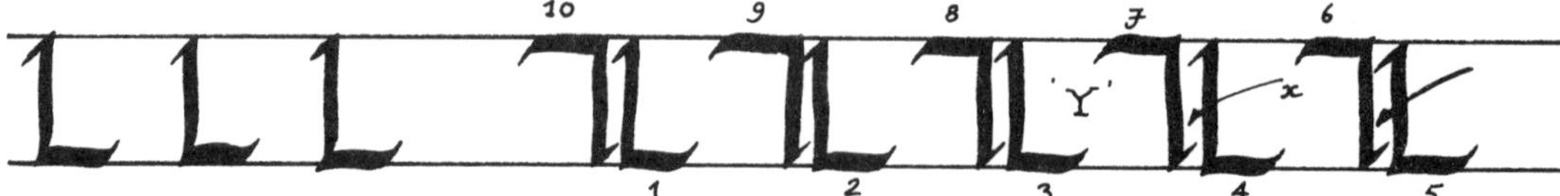

SPACE OUT THUS ~

TO MAKE THIS SEQUENCE FOLLOW THE NUMBERS. REVERSE THE PAPER TO WRITE 6-10. TRY TO MAKE THE SPACE 'X' EVEN THROUGHOUT THE PATTERN. SPACE 'Y' COULD BE USED FOR ADDITIONAL DECORATION.

INITIALS WITH AN INTERMEDIATE LEAF PATTERN.

THERE ARE MANY POSSIBLE VARIATIONS ON THIS IDEA.

y a b c d e f g

A COMBINATION USING TWO PENS.

amanuensisamanuensisam

WRITING ON BOTH SIDES OF A LINE.

USING 'a' HEIGHT LETTERS A DOUBLE BORDER CAN BE MADE. IF ASCENDERS ARE USED A DIFFERENT EFFECT CAN BE OBTAINED.

VaVbVc VVVV VAVBVc

THE V-SHAPE IS A USEFUL BORDER PATTERN. IF A WIDE NIB IS USED THERE WILL BE A SPACE WITHIN THE BORDER FOR LETTERS OR INITIALS LIKE THOSE SHOWN. THEY CAN BE EFFECTIVE IF WRITTEN IN A CONTRASTING COLOUR.

ONE WAY OF TURNING A CORNER.

COUNTER-CHANGED v's which are about two pen widths high.

SPACING between v's can alter the TEXTURE. Different spacing makes it easier to negotiate a curve.

THESE COULD BE REVERSED E'S OR C'S. NOTICE THE DIFFERENCE BETWEEN STROKES WHICH REMAIN APART AND THOSE WHICH OVERLAP.

EIEIEIE

A CORNER PIECE OR AN ELEMENT IN A LONG BORDER.

A BORDER MADE WITH TWO PENS AND THREE LINES OF WRITING. START AT THE OUTSIDE AND WORK INWARDS. TAKE CARE NOT TO SMUDGE AS YOU PROGRESS.

TRY USING A SECOND COLOUR FOR ALTERNATE LETTERS.

THIS PATTERN DOES NOT FIT INTO A CORNER NEATLY. INVENT ANOTHER CORNER PIECE TO SUIT THIS PATTERN.

USE A SECOND COLOUR FOR THE CORNER PIECE.

WHEN YOU DECIDE UPON THE WIDTH

H·H·H· H·H·H· H·H·H·

fine broad medium

OF A BORDER SELECT A SUITABLE NIB FOR ITS EXECUTION. WHICH NIB WOULD YOU CHOOSE FOR THIS EXAMPLE?

THE SPACES WITHIN A SCROLL CAN ALSO BE DECORATED.

A sequence can tell a story.

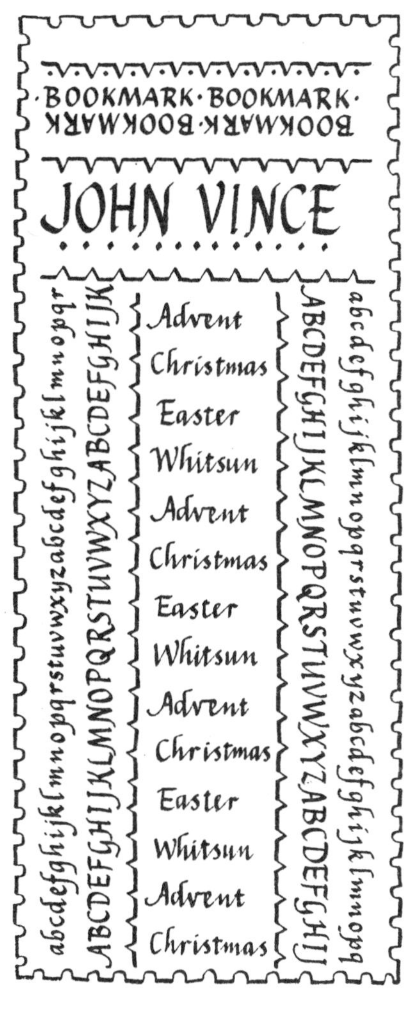

JEFFREY FLEET.

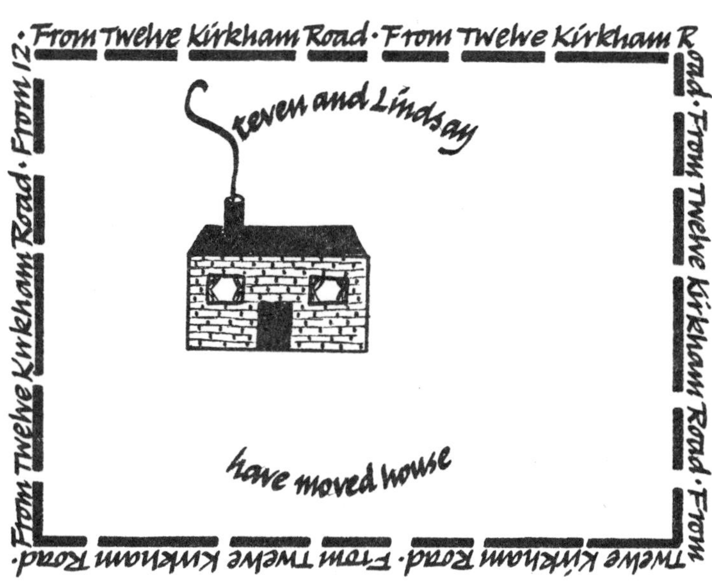

LINDSAY PENNY

TAILPIECE

The examples above show the work of two mature students who have developed their skills by following some of the ideas demonstrated in these pages. Calligraphy does require patience & a certain determination not to be discouraged when things do not work out in the way intended. Musicians need to practise each day & it is a good habit for calligraphers to adopt. Daily confrontation with a blank page does not need to become prolonged. Fifteen minutes a day can be quite effective. Practice sessions can best concentrate on just a few letter shapes or joins, rather than a prose passage chosen at random.

A short daily practice is better than an hour once a week.

NOTES ON USEFUL PENS

ARTPEN, Rotring: This range of pens has four widths. Cartridges can be used, but a filler unit is available. There is a good selection of coloured inks. These pens have a good grip & are well balanced. They make effective dip pens.

ARTPEN 1·9 artefacts berol italic IS MADE IN SIX COLOURS

BEROL · The 'Italic Pen' has a nib width of 2mm. Pens are sold singly, or in sets of~black~blue~dark blue~brown~green~red. The colours are strong & many of the exercises in this book will be enhanced by their use. The barrel is wide & has a good grip. These pens are fluent in use & the fibre tips seem durable.

A.T.CROSS · The 'Grey' range includes an italic nib. These very high quality pens have cartridges or can be fitted with a filler unit. The nib produces the best results if used on the 'back edge' thus~

back just four p.w.h.

OSMIROID · These pens probably have the widest range of nibs which include the useful Shadow nibs. The finer nibs will wear out at a faster rate, but they still represent good value. Cartridges or filler units can be used. Osmiroid nibs were used for many of the exercises shown above.

aceh B10 HIGH B6

PARKER · Several ranges include italic nibs but they seem rather wide for everyday use & make writing too large. Gold or steel nibs are available. The latter may be rather too firm for those with a 'light' touch. Gold nibs cost more but they are 'softer' in use. Most of the author's Parkers have been ground down to 1/32"~ see Penfriend below.

STANDARD 1mm. NIB

aE aand cmm ground nib 1/32 INCH

A SMALL DIFFERENCE IN NIB WIDTH CHANGES THE LETTER PROPORTIONS.

SHEAFFER: Different sets of 'Calligraphy' pens are available – in three widths. Cartridges are available in several colours. A great advantage of these pens for the beginner is the broad barrel which is comfortable to hold – always use the pen with the cap attached to provide 'balance'.

CALLIGRAPHY BROAD

sheaffer BOLD

FELT PENS with edged nibs are made by several companies. The quality is variable. Some of the most useful examples are the 5mm. versions which are useful for practice & bold work. The texture of a felt nib will often leave an irregular outline at the end of a stroke.

FELT W

TECHNICAL PENS which make a line of constant thickness are useful additions to the calligrapher's stock. The ·35 & ·5 sizes can be used for borders & decorations.

PENFRIEND

More expensive pens do require servicing or repair from time to time. Advice on pen selection, repairs & alterations are available on a personal basis from Roy Zeff, Penfriend Ltd., 7-8 Newbury St., London EC1A 7HX. (01-606-6542)

Most of the commentary in this book was completed with a Parker nib ground down with exactitude by Roy Zeff.

BIBLIOGRAPHY

Author	Title	Publisher	Year
Angel, Marie	The art of calligraphy	Hale	1985
Barnard, T & Jarman, C	Making calligraphy work for you	Osmiroid	1985
Bain, George	Celtic art: the methods of construction	Constable	1977
Benson, J.H	The first writing book – Arrighi's Operina	Oxford	1955
Burgoyne, P.A	Cursive handwriting	Dryad	1955
Child, Heather	Calligraphy today	Studio Vista	1976
" "	The calligrapher's handbook	Black	1986
" " et al	More than fine writing	Pelham	1986
Day, L.F	Alphabets old & new	Batsford	1910
Drogin, M	Medieval calligraphy	Prior	1980
Ehrlich, E	Nil desperandum	Hale	1985
Gourdie, Tom	Handwriting for today	Black	1971
" "	Improve your handwriting	"	1975
" "	Basic calligraphic hands	"	1984
" "	Mastering calligraphy	Search Press	1987
Irwin, K.G	Man learns to write	Dobson	1956
Johnston, Edw.	Writing illuminating & lettering	Pitman	1932

Neugebauer, F	The mystic art of written forms	Neugebauer	1980
Sassoon, R	The practical guide to lettering & applied calligraphy	Thames/Hudson	'85
Shepherd, M	The calligraphy sourcebook	Guild	1986
Thompson, T	The ABC of our alphabet	Studio	1942
Vince, John	Old Farms†	Murray	1982
" "	Power before steam†	"	1985

† Books written by hand which provide sources of further ideas

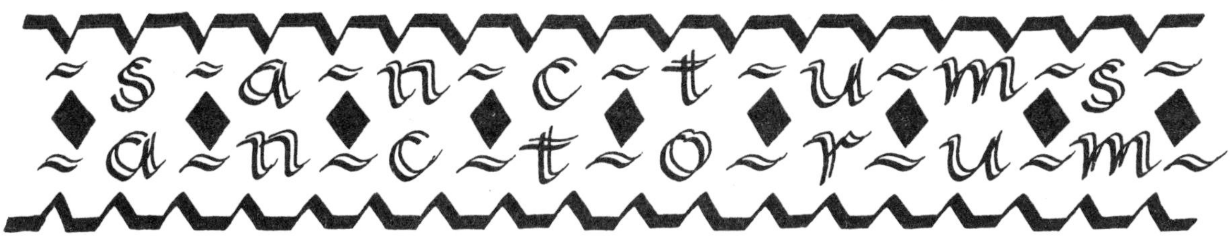

Enthusiasts are recommended to join
THE SOCIETY FOR ITALIC HANDWRITING
Secretary: Eric Vickers, M.A., Ph.D.,
80 Greenleaf Gardens, Polegate, East Sussex, BN26 6PH.

QUILLS & other calligraphic materials can be obtained from
The Universal Penman, Pitstone, Leighton Buzzard, Beds.
LU7 9AF.

(s.a.e. for catalogue)

abbreviations 21
address card 153
Agnus Dei 104
Aku Aku 110
Alleluia 136
alphabet 14
ampersands 78.96.150
Apple Fall 38
Ark 30
Balance 94
Basin 46
blue pencils 23
Bookmarks 132-5
Bookplates 130
Boomerang 42
Borders 148-51
Candles 58
capitals 18, 42, 66, 72, 80, 90, 126
Car 40
Car Park 114
Cats 36
Christmas Tree 136
colour, use of 104. 124. 128. 130. 136-41
commas 16
Corn Dolly 76
corrections 22
Cottage Loaf 60
Cup & Saucer 28
curves 22. 34. 96. 102
cushion 12
digging-in 11
dip pens 23
dots 16
Drain 48
Easter Island 110
Egg Cup 62
Elephant 128
Elms 108
false joins 15
Family Tree 146
Fishes 32. 84
Football 80
Grace 144
Greeting Cards 40. 58. 68. 74. 78. 100. 136.
grid, using a 22
Hallelujah 136
Hill Climb 78
Hop Scotch 86
Horseshoe 68
ink flow 12
Jack 70
joins 15
Jug 34
Junk 52
Keyhole 24
Landscapes 138
leaf forms 108
leather 70

left-handed 11.16
Longship 126
Maps 142
Marmite 92
Message in a Bottle 118
minuscules 14
Mitre 100
Monoliths 90
numerals 20
nut 74
Onion 116
Ouch 98
outline templates 116
overlaps 76.98.112
paper 13
Pax Vobis 134
Pebbles 82
Peeler's Hat 25
Penfriend 155
pen grip 9
Penny Farthing 106
pens, notes on 154-5
pen widths 21
Policeman 27
Porcus 66
posture 10
p.w.h. 21
quills 157
reduction 144
Reversing the image 133 135
Seagull 96
Soc. for Italic Handwriting 157
Sosban 26
Spanner 74
Spirals 102
Staddle Stone 124
Stonehenge 112
stops 16
Sunhat 31
Swan 122
symmetrical shapes 92
Teapot 64
Teepee 56
Tomahawk 54
Topiary 120
Troy Horse 88
Tug 50
Weathercock 44
Whiteleaf 72
Windmill 29
writing surface 12

HEKLA·PELEE
VESUVIUS·STR
OMBOLI·POPOCATE
PETL·KRAKATOA·
KILIMANJARO·ETNA·
NO SMOKING

I·COCK·UP·MY·FINGER·
I lay down my thumb
I·GIVE·YOU·THRICE·WAR
NING·Whenever I run A
HALFPENNY·PLATE·A penny
platter WHEN·I·COUNT·THRI
CE·I'll make you all scatter ~ 1-2-3-